THE FAITH-SHARING CONGREGATION

Developing a Strategy for the Congregation as Evangelist

Roger K. Swanson and Shirley F. Clement

DISCIPLESHIP RESOURCES

PO BOX 340003 • NASHVILLE, TN 37203-0003

www.discipleshipresources.org

Fourth printing: 2008

Cover design by Studiohaus

Library of Congress Catalog Card No. 95-69440

ISBN 978-0-88177-153-4

DR153

S. Readdean

CONTENTS

In Appreciation

We wish to express our appreciation for
congregations that nurtured us as we served them;
for colleagues who offered us friendship
and challenged us to excellence;
for United Methodist annual conferences,
where we tried out many of the concepts in this book;
for Church of the Servant, Oklahoma City
and its senior minister, Norman Neaves,
who offered us hospitality and inspiration.
We wish to express special appreciation
for Beverly Swanson, wife to Roger Swanson,
and friend to Shirley Clement,
for her support and constructive critique.

INTRODUCTION

This book is written for pastors of mainline congregations and those with whom they share leadership and responsibility. We offer here a local church strategy for doing evangelism that is biblical, contemporary, and theologically grounded in historic evangelicalism. The key is the congregation!

"The central, focal expression of ministry and mission in the name of Christ is found in the local church congregation," wrote the bishops of The United Methodist Church in a 1990 pastoral letter.[1] There is, as there has always been, great diversity in congregations. The congregation at Corinth, for instance, was remarkably different from the congregation at Jerusalem or Ephesus.

The same differences are apparent today. Some differences are denominational. Yet sometimes congregations of the same denomination, even within sight of one another, can differ vastly. Size is a contributing factor to this diversity, as are location, lifestyle, and the longevity of lay and clerical leadership. What is the same, however, is that each congregation gathers regularly to celebrate worship. In addition each congregation has a particular personality or culture that sets a pattern for conduct, outlook, and ultimately for growth or decline. Style of worship is a factor, as is the trust and rapport between the pastor and the people. Other factors would include vision, spirituality, liveliness, and whether that congregation is optimistic or discouraged about its future.

---

[1] *Vital Congregations, Faithful Disciples* (Nashville: Graded Press, 1990) p. 10.

Another common element in congregations that plays a major role in any strategy for evangelism is what the congregation perceives as its central purpose or its "primary task."[2] Sometimes this primary task is carefully thought out; other times it is intuitively demonstrated. There are congregations with small memberships that understand themselves as training schools for pastors in their first appointment. Others see their primary role in terms of children, or youth, or older adults. Central to the strategy for evangelism that this book promotes is an understanding of the primary task as faith development and faith deployment. What is primary, in other words, is what happens to people as the result of their participation in the congregation. How are they received and initiated into the church's fellowship? How is their faith formed and nurtured? How are they sent out into their daily lives to serve as disciples of Jesus? The illustration below is how this primary task might be portrayed.

Primary Task Illustration

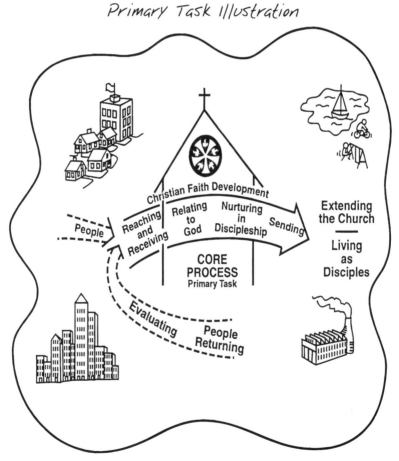

Used with permission from Discipleship Resources, Nashville, TN

---

[2] For a full discussion of primary task see James D. Anderson and Ezra Earl Jones *The Management of Ministry* (Nashville: Discipleship Resources, 1993), pp. 107-131.

This book is about how congregations evangelize and seek disciples. The first Christian community, not counting the Twelve Apostles, was the three thousand baptized on Pentecost. Of them the evangelist Luke says, "They devoted themselves to the apostles' teaching and fellowship, to the breaking of bread and the prayers" (Acts 2:42). *Kerygma* and *koinonia* were present with that first body of believers. The *kerygma* is the Christian message that was present in the apostles' teaching. This message proclaimed Christ's coming in the flesh, his teaching about the kingdom of God, his atonement for sin, his resurrection, and all the benefits thereof to the world in general and to believers in particular. The same Christian *kerygma* is present today in preaching and teaching: Bible studies, Sunday school classes, and other instructional venues. Prayer and worship were also vital. The congregation described in Acts 2:42, like the disciples at Emmaus, recognized and experienced Christ in breaking the bread of Holy Communion. Christian formation occurs today as persons learn to practice the disciplines of daily prayer and worship and to participate in the corporate worship of the larger community.

The *koinonia* is the fellowship among and between Christians. It cannot be shoved aside because of a crowded schedule or for any other reason. The *kerygma* without the *koinonia* is unfinished; the *koinonia* without the *kerygma* is inadequate. Those first Christians in Jerusalem were bound together into a community by a common experience of Word and sacrament. People were in relationship, not only with God through Jesus Christ but also with one another through Jesus Christ. People were welcomed as sisters and brothers in Christ. They were made to feel at home. The culture and climate, in other words, was conducive to community.

The author Madeleine L'Engle says it succinctly:

> *We hear a lot about evangelism today and how the church must pay more attention to it. But mostly evangelism is not what we tell people, unless what we tell is totally consistent with who we are. It is who we are that is going to show the love that brought us all into being, that cares for us, now and forever. If we do not have love in our hearts, our words of love will have little meaning.*[3]

The strategy for doing evangelism in and through the local congregation focuses on the congregation's life together as well as on particular ministries. We call this strategy "the faith-sharing congregation." Five principles nurture and support this strategy:

---

[3] Madeleine L Engle. *The Rock That is Higher* (Wheaton, Ill.:Harold Shaw Publishers, 1993), p 166.

1. Evangelism is not one option among several that a local congregation can choose to act upon. What God has done and is doing for the world through Jesus Christ needs to be told to as many people as possible, as often as possible, in as many ways as possible.

2. Evangelism is the work of all the people, clergy and laity, working together. Evangelism is not the prerogative of the clergy. Baptism, not ordination, gives a Christian authority for the work of ministry.

3. The personality or culture of a congregation is as important for the work of evangelism as any specific ministry of evangelism. People join churches today, not according to brand label, but on the basis of being welcomed, nurtured, and challenged. No matter how orthodox a pastor's Christology may be and how passionately he or she preaches, a negatively-charged atmosphere can undo his or her best efforts.

4. The work of evangelism is best served, not by lifting up evangelism, but by focusing on the congregation's primary task of faith formation. Christ is the one we must lift up, not a particular task or committee of the church.

5. The near future of the Christian enterprise rests with re-invigorated congregational life. We may speak of the church and mean the universal church of Christ. People, however, are found by Christ and grow in Christ within local congregations. Furthermore, the denomination of a local congregation is diminishing in importance. Whether people are welcomed, fed, and equipped for ministry within its fellowship is what is important. A strategy for doing evangelism in the local congregation is therefore critical.

Experience and conviction combine to promote within the pages that follow a threefold faith-sharing strategy for evangelism that includes:

- sharing faith through the practice of genuine hospitality;
- sharing faith through relationships and personal story;
- sharing faith through the "domestic" church of the family however it is constituted.

THE FAITH-SHARING CONGREGATION

A popular television program in the 1950s, titled "To Tell the Truth" challenged a panel of theatrical celebrities to differentiate between the genuine article and an imitation. Three persons would be introduced to the panel, each of whom claimed to be the exact same person, working at the same profession or vocation. Probing questions were asked of each in an effort to sort out which one of the three was telling the truth. At the end of each segment, the celebrity contestants voted on their choices, and the "real" person was asked to stand up.

WHO IS THE "REAL" EVANGELIST?

In the New Testament only Philip (Acts 21:8) and Timothy (2 Timothy 4:5) are specifically identified as evangelists. The one other reference to the "office" of evangelist occurs in Ephesians 4:11 in the list of the varied leadership offices through which God will gift the church. These offices also include apostles, prophets, pastors, and teachers. In a study of leadership roles in the early church, Eugene S. Wehrli reports that "evangelist is to be the new term for leaders in the church that function similarly to the original apostles."[4] As the title would indicate, the first evangelists were preachers of the gospel, the evangel. Their responsibilities, along with other leaders, was "to equip the saints for the work of ministry, for building up the body of Christ" (Ephesians 4:12). The role of the evangelist, then, from what we read of Philip and Timothy, involved both personal witness and public proclamation.

---

[4] Eugene S. Wehrli. *Gifted By Their Spirit: Leadership Roles in the New Testament* (Cleveland: Pilgrim Press, 1992), p 29.

You will remember Philip's encounter with the Ethiopian on the way to Gaza (Acts 8:26-39), which resulted in the baptism of the Ethiopian. Paul urged Timothy to "proclaim the message; be persistent whether the time is favorable or unfavorable; convince, rebuke, and encourage, with the utmost patience in teaching" (2 Timothy 4:2).

THE PASTOR AS EVANGELIST

These references to Philip and Timothy suggest that it is the local church pastor who carries major responsibility for evangelism. Many lay people are not confident enough of their own witness and are often reluctant to regard their neighbors as "unchurched." They are glad to leave evangelism to the clergy. Pastors, whether ordained or licensed, are expected to lead congregations in mediating Christ's saving presence. They do this through fulfilling three historic leadership roles: word, sacrament, and order.[5] The work of a pastor is to be a communicator, community organizer, and trainer for the work of ministry. As a trainer the pastor helps to equip the congregation and its laity for the mission of witness and service in the world. Pastors also play a central role in helping to form and nurture a community of belonging. The sacraments are the most important occasions when such Christian community is formed. A key role, however, in transmitting the gospel is the pastor's role as communicator, as a herald of the good news.

The first occurrence in the New Testament of the root word for evangelism and evangelist, the Greek *eu aggelia* or "good message," is found in the announcement of the angel to shepherds near Bethlehem on the night Jesus was born. Does this make the angel the first evangelist? The message was, "'Do not be afraid; for see—I am bringing you good news of great joy for all the people'" (Luke 2:10). "[F]aith comes," writes the apostle Paul, "from what is heard" (Romans 10:17). Pastors are expected to be instruments that enable hearing as they articulate the good news in preaching and teaching and thus lead persons toward the Christ who is moving toward them.

"Evangelism is what we do," writes George Hunter, "to make the Christian faith, life, and mission a live option for undiscipled people."[6] To the degree that pastors confess the Christian faith personally, publicly proclaim its good news with conviction, and call persons to commitment to Jesus Christ as Lord and Savior, they indeed function as evangelists in the best sense of that word. "Defining evangelism as the verbal proclamation of the gospel,"

---

[5] *The Book of Discipline of The United Methodist Church—2004*(Nashville: The United Methodist Publishing House, 2004), ¶ 303.

[6] George G. Hunter III. *The Contagious Congregation* (Nashville: Abingdon, 1979), p. 26.

William J. Abraham says, "provides a clear, manageable concept that is rooted in the early history of the word and that calls the church to excellence in communicating the Christian gospel to those who are prepared to listen."[7]

Defining evangelism by the preaching function also fits the office of evangelist as it exists in the church today. Evangelists, in the minds of most people, are not the pastors of local congregations. They are traveling preachers (if only as far as a television studio) who with varying doses of "fire and brimstone," cajole potential converts "to flee from the wrath to come." This is mostly a caricature. Itinerant evangelists have played a key role in the propagation of the faith. Francis of Assisi is included in their company, as would be most of the circuit riders in frontier America. Each year evangelist Billy Graham is identified in national polls as one of the most respected persons in the country. Lesser known but equally responsible men and women have felt themselves called to the ministry of evangelism and, at significant sacrifice, have made themselves available to God and church. The focus of many of these journeyman evangelists has been the renewal of local congregations. To that end they have served with effectiveness and distinction.

THE LAITY AS EVANGELIST

Nevertheless, the most effective evangelists of Christ are the church's laity. This has been the case since the beginning. In Acts 8:4 we find that it was not the apostles who first took the gospel out from Jerusalem but those lay persons who were evicted from the city following the martyrdom of Stephen.[8] In Corinth Paul experienced the gracious hospitality of a lay couple, Priscilla and Aquila (Romans 16:3). They housed a church in their home and, by Paul's own words, "risked their necks for my life" (Romans 16:4). On the American frontier the circuit riders get most of the space in the history books, but when they were off planting new congregations it was the laity who nurtured the growing church and invited their friends and neighbors to join them. Michael Green writes of these lay missioners in every century and circumstance: "They went everywhere gossiping the gospel; they did it naturally, enthusiastically, and with the conviction of those who are not paid to say that sort of thing. Consequently, they were taken seriously, and the movement spread, notably among the lower classes."[9]

---

[7] William J. Abraham, *The Logic of Evangelism* (Grand Rapids, Michigan: William B. Eerdmans Publishing Company, 1989), pp. 44,45.

[8] In Acts 8:1 we are told that following Stephen s death "all except the apostles were scattered throughout the countryside of Judea and Samaria." Acts 8:4 says that "those who were scattered went from place to place, proclaiming the word."

[9] Michael Green, *Evangelism in the Early Church* (Grand Rapids, Michigan: William B. Eerdmans Publishing Company, 1970), p. 173.

Evangelists are, for the most part, people—whether laity or clergy doesn't matter—who lead other people to a living faith in God through Jesus Christ. The *ekklesia* or gathered congregation, however, also plays a central role, often overlooked, in evangelizing or heralding Christ. This role is carried out in the quality of its life together. We call it "the faith-sharing congregation."

A faith-sharing congregation is one in which there is an "evangelical flow." People with passion for the good news flow into, through, and out from congregations in intentional ministry and mission. They come into such a congregation because of a hospitality system that reaches out to them wherever they are and welcomes them as they are. In their increasing involvement in congregational life, they are related to God and nurtured in discipleship. Central to this process is an equipping of people to share their personal faith with others within their social networks. People go out from the faith-sharing congregation with the intention to serve God and their neighbor. The first place to which disciples return, motivated by faith sharing, is, we believe, the family. That which makes a family more loving and just carries with it an invitation: "Come to Christ."

The effectiveness of the laity in evangelism is partly due to the fact that there are far more lay men and women than clergy. Laity also have more access to people in family relationships, in the neighborhood, and in the work place. The truth is every study shows that when asked who played the most significant role in their faith journey, people will occasionally list pastors and evangelists; more often they list lay persons: friends, relatives, and neighbors. Most frequently mentioned are mothers, grandparents, fathers, spouses, children, Sunday school teachers, and college roommates, in that order. Recent research shows that of ten new persons who come to a church and stay, nine were brought by a lay friend. What do these persons all have in common? The power of example! We live with these people up close and personal. We know them and they know us intimately. (They love us anyway!) We trust them. When asked what makes such persons winsome witnesses of Christ, people often say, "they practice what they preach."

Probably the most effective and organized lay ministry of evangelism, ecumenically and internationally is the Lay Witness Mission. Founded in 1963 on the premise that lay persons would often "hear" the gospel in the faith stories of other laity in ways that they would not "hear" it from clergy, the Lay Witness Mission is still going strong and has for many congregations been a turning point toward revitalized and more intentional ministries of witness and outreach. More than 1500 clergy by their own word have come to ordained ministry through the influence of a Lay Witness Mission. One hears other stories of laity finding it easier to share their faith after such a mission in their congregation, and the ripple effect of their witness in church, family, and community.

As effective as their witness is, the numbers of laity who intentionally and self-consciously share their faith in Jesus Christ is sadly limited. This is due, in no small measure, to the negligence of pastors and other congregational leaders in training the laity for personal witness. Sermons telling the laity what they "ought" to be doing are irresponsible if not followed up with basic training in personal faith sharing.

The work of an evangelist is to share faith in God's gracious intent in Jesus Christ, through personal witness and public proclamation. That work is carried on by the baptized, whether lay, clergy, or called specifically to the office of evangelist.

THE CONGREGATION AS EVANGELIST

It is so often at this point, after identifying the work of pastors, evangelists, and the laity, that the discussion of who serves as evangelist typically ends. Evangelism is seen as one individual encountering another. Or it is seen as one pastor or evangelist heralding Christ in a sanctuary or revival tent. We think of evangelism as "personal work." What is not accounted for is how much evangelism is done not by individuals but by congregations as Christ's people living out together what they believe and teach. Early Christian leaders understood the dynamic of congregational environment when it came to the gospel of God's love in Christ. They understood that in the pagan culture of the Roman Empire Christians had to do more than "talk the talk." They had to demonstrate love "in truth and action" (John 3:18): "[Y]ou are a letter of Christ," wrote Paul to a congregation, "prepared by us, written not with ink but with the Spirit of the living God" (2 Corinthians 3:3). "When unchurched people walk into our building, they're at a different starting point than the unchurched of fifty years ago," observed two of the pastors at Eastside Church in Kirkland, Washington. "The truly unchurched are thoroughgoing relativists, have taken pluralism to its absurd limit, and cannot conceive how Scripture could be authoritative in their life. They need a safe and often long preconversion stage in which they build confidence in us, establish the authority of Scripture, and cement relationships. We have to honor that phase. Unchurched people today distrust church, and they need to come and just watch us for a while."[10]

---

[10] Doug Murren and Mike Meeks, "How Your Church Can Evangelize," *Leadership* magazine (Summer 1995), p. 93.

The vision that God has given many congregational leaders in our time is a re-invigorated congregational life, centered in and reflecting Christ's character and compassion for the world. A particular form of that vision of the vital congregation is of the congregation as evangelist, what we are calling "the faith-sharing congregation."

A case may be made that the New Testament says much more about the corporateness of the church community than it does of the solitary Christian. Western Christianity has applied the term *you*, whenever it occurs in Scripture, to a single individual, as in, "And remember, I am with you always, to the end of the age" (Matthew 28:20), or "You are the light of the world" (Matthew 5:14). Although deeply personal in its focus and application, Christianity runs the risk of being too personal if it overlooks or excludes the congregation, the community, and the world. References to *you* in the Gospels are usually meant to be plural. They need to be applied to the community of the disciples or to the church that followed.

This is most evident in the two primary images of the church that occur in the New Testament: the people of God and the body of Christ. Both are corporate images. In 1 Peter 2, thought to be part of a sermon for baptismal candidates, the church is presented as the "new" Israel. What was said of the old Israel (Exodus 19:5) is said of the church: "But you are a chosen race, a royal priesthood, a holy nation, God's own people" (1 Peter 2:9). The stress here is on corporateness—not what believers are one by one, but what they are together.

Seeing the church as the body of Christ makes the point even more clear. "The body does not consist of one member but of many," (1 Corinthians 12:14) reasons the apostle Paul. As within human anatomy, so with the church: no one part or individual can be effective alone—"If one member suffers, all suffer together" (1 Corinthians 12:26). Christ promises "where two or three are gathered in my name, I am there among them" (Matthew 18:20).

To put it another way, any local church or congregation is greater than the sum of its parts. It has an identity to which everyone contributes and which is more than everyone together. That identity is more than denomination, or region, or neighborhood.

Local reputation may come close to revealing true identity; integrity is often more apparent to persons outside the congregation. Late in the afternoons of several days each month a UPS delivery person made a stop at a particular church. "I can't quite put my finger on it," he said one day to the church receptionist, "but there is something different about this church. It's comfortable; I almost feel like the building welcomes me every time I come." What he experienced was something corporate and environmental. The delivery person experienced the congregation even when the congregation wasn't there! "I'm going to have to come some Sunday," he often said on leaving. He felt welcomed and invited to come.

What is your congregation's reputation? Using United Methodists as an example, a church may have a reputation among pastors either as a preferred appointment, or one to avoid. Much more important for faith sharing is how your church is perceived within the community it seeks to serve. That information is available from barbers and hairdressers, police, gas station attendants, at city hall, and at the chamber of commerce. "If you are young and religious," said a downtown store owner in a county seat town about one congregation, "whatever's happening is happening there." It sounded interesting and inviting. Another congregation was identified not for the down-and-outers but for the "up and inners." How a congregation is perceived in the community often comes very close to what a congregation essentially is.

CULTURAL SHIFT

Thinking of the congregation corporately helps us understand and deal with a major shift in cultural attitudes about church and congregation. This shift has taken two forms. First, a church's denomination does not have the "pull" it had a generation ago. At that time, even many of the unchurched could identify with a denomination with which they did not actively affiliate. If later such persons came to faith or encountered personal need, they would come into the denomination of their parents and grandparents. Such does not seem to be the case today. The futurist Joel Barker says that when the paradigm shifts everything goes back to zero.[11] Mainline denominations have no advantage in today's religious climate. People are looking for community and belonging, not for a heritage and history. A denomination label at one time could make up for a lot of congregational deficiencies. This is not so today. Pastors know that they cannot grow a church today on transfers from their own denomination. The quality of life within a congregation matters much more than what the sign outside reads.

The other form this cultural shift has taken is that people are not as conventionally membership-minded as they once were. For a few years after World War II, joining a local congregation had as much to do with assimilating into the political, economic, and social community as it did with identifying with a particular religious association. People today are much more tuned in to satisfaction in personal relationships than membership in most anything. The number of couples living without benefit of formal

---

[11] Joel A. Barker, "The Power of Vision" (Discovering the Future Video Series, Charthouse International Learning Corporation, Burnsville, MN).

marriage vows is further evidence of increasing anti-traditionalist attitudes in our culture. As with living together, many people today see attendance and support but not formal affiliation to be all the commitment they are willing to handle.

And yet the same deep inner yearning for God that characterizes human life this side of Eden is equally as evident. Some things do not change. Human hearts are still restless until they rest in God. Congregations that are welcoming, flexible, genuine, and patient in love will not lack for seekers after God at their doors and in their pews. Such faith-sharing congregations, no matter where they occur and what their size might be, are typically focused on the quality of their life and ministry together. A word visitors sometimes use to describe such a congregation is "delightful." To understand what this specifically means, we need to focus on the culture and primary task of the faith-sharing congregation.

CULTURE OF THE CONGREGATION

Webster's dictionary defines culture in sociological terms as "the concepts, habits, skills, art, instruments, institutions of a given people in a given period."[12] Culture is what is unique about a particular group of people. It has roots in the history of the group, from which traditions arise, but it is also developing continually as the group meets new situations. Some church leaders talk about climate. Culture is more inclusive. It includes both the visible and the invisible, both the attitudes and the actions the congregation has taken in the past as well as currently.

Culture is important within business organizations. Seventy percent of all business problems have been identified as either people-related or culturally based. "By not focusing on the workplace culture as the source for transforming the business," writes Edward M. Marshall, "we have missed the proverbial forest for the trees."[13]

A church with its own unique culture is exemplified by First United Methodist Church in Alexandria, Louisiana. That congregation has a very welcoming environment, particularly to those persons who appreciate good art. It is part of the culture of the congregation. Art work adorns hallways. Sculpture can be seen in several specially designed niches. The sanctuary, as you would expect, is particularly stimulating, with modern sculpture and art challenging the worshiper to inquire about the contemporary relevance of the ancient word. Another congregation's culture in the mid-west mirrors the informal, down-to-earth values of the rural community it has served for more than a century, with many of the families going back to the beginning days of the church.

---

[12] The *Webster's New Universal Unabridged Dictionary*, Second Edition (Dorset & Baber 1983), p. 444.
[13] Edward M. Marshall, "The Collaborative Workplace," Management Review, (June 1995), p. 15.

Culture is that sum total of a congregation which is more than the constituent parts.

Factors that play a major role in shaping congregational culture, or climate, according to W. James Cowell, include mutuality, expectancy, trust, flexibility, positive self-image, spiritual commitment, and optimism. The physical plant also plays a critical role.[14] To this list could be added vision, mission, leadership, hospitality, and service to the larger community beyond the walls of the congregation.

It should be evident that lack of the above factors also contributes to the culture of the congregation in a negative way. Stephen Gunter, on the faculty of Candler School of Theology, has been quoted as deliberately misspelling a verse from the King James Version of the Bible, "Where there is no vision, the people *parish*"[15] (Proverbs 29:18). Too often a parish has become a confined unit beyond which the congregation seems unwilling to move out in mission.

A newcomer to a particular community attended a congregation in a nearby city one Sunday morning. A staff member of the congregation he had visited responded quickly with a telephone call, expressing pleasure at his visit but also informing him not to expect a newcomer visit. The staff member offered to send a packet of material through the mail, but home visits were not for persons that far from their church building. He closed the conversation inviting the newcomer to come again. The newcomer wondered why he should attend that church if his home was too "far out" for a welcoming visit. The newcomer's nearby community was not part of the congregation's *parish*, as the staff person understood it. John Wesley's "the world is my parish" has become in many places, "the parish is my world!"

A further discussion of congregational culture follows in Chapters 2 and 3, with a focus on the one value we choose to identify as critical to the faith-sharing congregation, namely hospitality.

THE PRIMARY TASK

Another way of focusing on the quality of a congregation's life is to identify and work on what we have previously called the "primary task" of the congregation. A contemporary Christian hymn celebrates that "the church is a people."[16] As discussed on previous pages, the primary image of the church in the New

---

[14] W. James Cowell, Extending Your Congregation s Welcome (Nashville: Discipleship Resources, 1989), pp. 8-16.

[15] W. Stephen Gunter is the Arthur J. Moore Professor of Evangelism at Candler School of Theology, Emory University, Atlanta, Georgia. Norman Neaves, pastor of Church of the Servant (UMC) in Oklahoma City, offered the quote in an interview with the authors.

[16] Richard K. Avery and Donald S. March, "We Are the Church," The United Methodist Hymnal (Nashville: The United Methodist Publishing House, 1989) p. 558.

Testament is corporate. There is more, however. The church is people with a particular passion and mission. The church is a people under the mandate to "[g]o therefore and make disciples of all nations" (Matthew 28:19). The church's identity is determined by its task. Congregations have work to do. But what is primary and what is peripheral in that work?

Your congregation is a system, comprised of a large number of processes. In this respect it is not dissimilar to a human being. The physical human organism is comprised of a number of processes. Some deal with reproduction, others with metabolism, others with the operation of the five senses, to mention only three. In the congregation there is a membership process, carefully thought out or simply acted out, but there, nevertheless. There are also processes that determine how worship is planned and achieved, how Sunday school teachers are recruited, how the annual budget is assembled and underwritten, and so forth. Struggling congregations often have not thought through these processes. Instead they focus on problems to be solved as quickly and with as little pain as possible.

Much is to be learned, however, by analyzing these processes, and identifying the "core" process, that one without which all the others possess no unity. As a beginning, one may understand that a process has three parts: input, transformation, and output. It might be pictured as in the figure below.

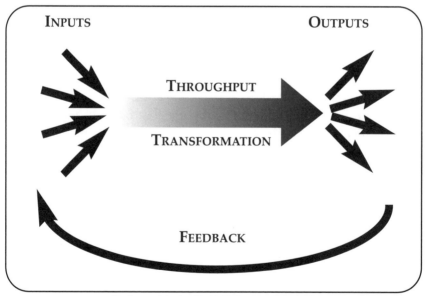

Used by permission from Discipleship Resources, Nashville, TN.

The human system has its core process, made up of many processes. The input of food and drink is transformed into energy for operating all other systems. If this system fails to work properly, all other systems slow down or fail to operate. If the system should fail completely or food and drink be cut off entirely, death would result.

A neighborhood repair garage also has a core process. The input is your car. It is not functioning properly. It stalls at stop lights, or smokes excessively, or is leaking oil on the driveway. You want it fixed. The output desired is a car that can be driven trouble-free wherever you want to go. What happens between the input and the output is a kind of transformation. The mechanic listens to your complaint, studies the situation, makes a diagnosis, and corrects the problem. There are other processes in a garage. There are those associated with bookkeeping or with making major or minor repairs. There is a very important process having to do with ordering and taking delivery of parts. These processes, however, all serve the core process of receiving automobiles, repairing them, and returning them to their owners.

In days of corporation downsizing it is not difficult to imagine a congregation having to cut its ministry and mission budgets. Picture a group of leaders from a congregation holding a retreat at a conference center. Their task is to cut programs and save dollars. How, they wonder, can they go about their work? Can they eliminate one staff person? Can the secretary become part-time? Sunday school curriculum is expensive; does the Sunday school have to buy a new curriculum each year? What about the denomination's goals for mission? Can expectations be less than 100% of last year? You may be able to develop the scenario further; you may be living it at this very moment. Typically such task groups have a dollar figure in mind and cut a bit here and there until they are close enough to be comfortable. What they risk is cutting so close to the bone as to endanger the church's very purpose for being.

A better way of aligning a church budget with expected income would be to ask of the desired results. "What is the mission of the congregation? What do we hope for?" Such basic questions lead us closer to what is primary in the work of the church. Of all the processes in your congregation, what is the core process or primary task? Activities and programs alone are no answer. Is the purpose of the congregation to grow? Why? Is it to make disciples? What then? Such questions get to the heart of the issue. Is not the purpose of the faith community to make and grow Christians who will in turn benefit the community at large?

Think of the three parts of a process: input, transformation, and output. The input is people. The output also is people, people different from when they entered: people who have been welcomed, assimilated, and made disciples, and who go out to make a difference in their families, friendships, and communities. Between this particular input and the desired output is the transformation that occurs. Lives are changed by God's Spirit. One way to speak of the purpose and *primary task or core process* of the congregation is to see it as a process of *faith development.*

There are four identifiable functions within the primary task, or core process, of faith development.

1. People are invited by a friend or simply respond to their own yearnings for God. They approach a congregation, which rejoices in their coming and reaches out to welcome them.

2. People seek God through various settings in the congregation. They enter into a relationship with God through Jesus Christ, mediated through the various disciplines and practices they learn, such as Bible reading and study, worship, prayer, fasting, and attendance upon the Eucharist, the Holy Communion.

3. People are nurtured and encouraged to grow in their knowledge and understanding of the Christian faith, particularly as it interfaces with the secular world. This knowledge is not for the sake of knowledge, but that Christians may more fully live the abundant life in family and community, and may more confidently represent and witness to the faith they hold.

4. People move out of the congregation and into the world, aware that they are ministers and ambassadors of Christ, committed to witness and service in the world.

Adapted from GUIDELINES. Copyright 1997 by Abingdon Press. Reprinted by permission.

You will find another illustration of the primary task on page vi of the Introduction. In this illustration, the congregation is represented by the church building. People move into, through, and out from a congregation. What happens in steps 2 and 3 above determines the effectiveness of steps 1 and 4.

In the pages that follow, the culture and core process of the congregation will be explored because they are integral to our vision of a truly evangelical congregation, centered in the Center and with measurable results.

Based on extensive local church experience in "doing" evangelism, as well as on studying churches of different sizes and in a variety of settings, we are proposing this strategy:

1. Hospitality: congregations reach out to welcome persons, whether newcomers or others;
2. Individuals be equipped to share their personal faith story; (The people most readily available for this faith sharing will turn out to be friends, relatives, associates, and neighbors.)
3. Families be given the resources to serve one another as a primary faith community.

Each of the above represents a critical aspect of the core process of a congregation.

The next two chapters will focus on biblical and congregational hospitality, as people are reached out to and welcomed into the family of families called the congregation.

2

$\mathcal{S}$HARING $\mathcal{F}$AITH $\mathcal{T}$HROUGH $\mathcal{H}$OSPITALITY

"Home is the place where, when you have to go there,
They have to take you in."
Robert Frost, "The Death of the Hired Man"[17]

There are few places on this planet that are more hostile for human beings than deserts. The names of these great and terrible wasteland areas are etched in our minds: in Africa, the Sahara and the Kalahari; in North America, Death Valley; in Asia, the Gobi Desert; in Israel, the Judean wilderness to the west of the Jordan River. Often freezing at night, at midday a desert can drain a body of so much of its moisture it can be life-threatening. Many casual tourists and pilgrims have learned these realities the hard way. Although there is more "life" in a desert than might first appear, the sparse rainfall has created an ecology which cannot support a large human population.

People are few and far between in desert climates. They often live in small scattered settlements or in some places in nomadic bands. Travel is particularly dangerous. Even with the conveniences of modern transportation, prudence dictates that a person not set out on a journey of any consequence alone. In earlier times such travel was usually undertaken in caravans. In those times, however, and in many places still today, what every traveler could depend upon, whether journeying alone or in small groups, was a welcome along the way.

---

[17] Robert Frost. "The Death of the Hired Man," *Great American Poets,* (New York: Clarkson N. Potter, Inc. 1986). p. 19.

Thus the offer and gift of hospitality became and remains today the moral cornerstone of life together in desert communities. The Bedouins of the Sinai Peninsula and the Arabian Desert share many of the same experiences as the nomadic Israelites who traveled with Abraham or with Moses through the same regions. The practice of hospitality became the foundation of our Judeo-Christian tradition and heritage.

In the Book of Genesis, chapter 18, we read of the patriarch Abraham, who as the story goes, was sitting one day at the entrance to his goat-hide tent pitched on the edge of the Negeb desert. He saw three strangers approaching. Like all desert dwellers, he offered the travelers what he would wish to be offered, namely sanctuary and hospitality. Thus, the travelers received the shade of Abraham's tent for rest, water for washing away the dust of the journey, and a sumptuous feast.

Abraham offered the three strangers, in the best sense of the word, all the comforts of *home*. He and Sarah offered them a home away from home.

Hospitality is an offer of home and family to those who, at the moment and for all practical purposes, are homeless. "Make yourself at home," offers the gracious host or hostess. "Mi casa es su casa," is how the words translate in Spanish culture: "My house is your house."

Such hospitality touches every aspect of life. Indeed it becomes all the more genuine when we are reduced to our most basic needs. Traveling in modern Israel late one afternoon, a tourist/pilgrim found himself in need of just such hospitality. Standing in a crowded square in Nazareth waiting to enter the church that houses Mary's well, he was becoming increasingly uncomfortable. His charter flight to Israel had been delayed for twelve hours. On arriving in Tel Aviv, his tour group had immediately been boarded onto buses and taken on their first day of touring. By late afternoon he was exhausted and sick and in need of a rest room. The guide couldn't help, except to explain that there was no such facility anywhere nearby.

Somehow, by the grace of God, their conversation had been overheard. A man in the Bedouin headdress of a Palestinian spoke to him in one word, "Toilet?" "Yes! Toilet! Please! Where?" the traveler responded. The Palestinian man beckoned him to follow. Going down a labyrinth of ever-narrowing streets they came, finally, to a plain door which they entered. A moment later another door was opened which met the traveler's need. On leaving, the traveler ventured to thank his host. "Shalom!" he said, grateful for the peace the word conveyed. A broad smile enveloped his host's face. "Shalom!" he was offered in return. Was the host at peace, too, having met a basic obligation of his heritage and his faith? The traveler rejoined his group, refreshed, with an experience of biblical hospitality in the land of the Bible.

Now picture a more familiar setting. On the first Sunday morning in a new city a family set out for worship in a downtown church. Not finding a parking space immediately, the father dropped his family off in front of the church. Later when he tried to join them in a pew, he asked the woman sitting next to the aisle to excuse him. "And where do you think you're going?" she greeted him. He wanted to join his family, but she didn't want to be inconvenienced. She suggested that he look elsewhere and join his family after the service. They never returned to that church.

In your congregation are strangers offered the hospitality of home? Think about the experience of being a member of your congregation. For many people church is the one place, other than the family, where they experience the warmth of being welcomed home. People there know you and you know them, or at least a significant number of them. They are glad to see you, as you are glad to see them. You exchange news, catch up with each other's lives, support each other in common tasks and in times of need.

The essence of hospitality is to be known and welcomed, needed and loved.

Do you know specifically how other people experience your congregation? Strangers or newcomers have unique experiences. What of non-participating members? Many of our mainline congregations report as many as 50% of the congregation are marginal or inactive. Experience suggests that many members choose to remain peripheral and occasional attendees for the same reasons that visitors elect not to return.

You may want to test this for your congregation by setting up listening posts. Informally interview several persons who are fairly new to the congregation. Ask what their experience was and is in coming to the church. What meant the most when they first attended? The same listening would be valuable with marginal members and with those persons who visit but keep formal relationships with another congregation. More difficult but even more helpful, would be to follow the lead of industries who do "exit interviews" of employees leaving the company. This would be especially appropriate for those persons who transfer from one congregation to another in the same community.

So many of us in the church have lost the ability to be objective. We have become "church blind." We are either preoccupied with our place or task in the congregation, or have simply been a member and active participant for so long that we assume our experience of the friendliness of the congregation is or ought to be everyone's experience. If it isn't, it is "their" fault. How often have you heard it said in church that "friendliness is a two-way street; if strangers were themselves more friendly, they would find the congregation more friendly"? The same kind of subtle hostility is often heard in reference to marginal members. The problem is their commitment, not a failing of the congregation to be welcoming and hospitable.

In the 1950's Marshall McLuhan coined the phrase, "the medium is the message." We could also say that the mediator is the message. The Christian message is the good news of God's universal and bountiful grace to all persons everywhere. The mediator of this grace or generosity is Jesus Christ and none other. The earliest statements of the Christian *kerygma* or proclamation allowed no room for debate on this issue. "There is salvation in no one else," proclaimed the apostle Peter, "for there is no other name under heaven given among mortals by which we must be saved" (Acts 4:12). In Christ, therefore, God has not only announced God's love for creation but has, at great cost, redeemed that creation. In Christ nothing matters but God's generosity received by faith, not race or economic status, not nationality or sexuality, not whether a person is a charter member of a congregation or a stranger.

The medium is also the message in the local congregation. Indeed, this message, like the Word in John 1, means little unless it is incarnated and embodied in a welcoming congregation. How the congregation practices this good news of God's welcome is the real delivery of God's message, the gospel of Jesus Christ. No matter what the congregation has to offer in terms of an attractive facility, an able professional staff, exciting worship and programming for all ages, what people see and experience in a congregation is and will be the most powerful expression of good news.

A Christian congregation, (or a faith community of any kind—Bible study group, prayer group, service group) affirms and shares its faith in God through Jesus Christ, first and foremost, through the offer of hospitality to the strangers in its midst. There is no more effective witness to the universal offer of God's grace through Jesus Christ than a congregation offering a genuine welcome to persons whomever and wherever they are. In such a hospitable congregation there are no differences that make a difference, no "strangers and aliens" (Ephesians 2:18) but "one body through the cross" (Ephesians 2:16) of Jesus Christ.[18]

What people yearn to find in this life is, in the words of the poet-laureate of New England, Robert Frost, "a place where when you have to go there, they have to take you in." How fortunate we are if, when such a time comes, they want to take us in. How much does your congregation want to receive those who await a sincere welcome? Unfortunately, many people find no

---

[18] See a full discussion of this new humanity in Ephesians 2:11-21.

such welcome in the church or in the community. Modern life, for many people, feels like a desert environment through which they wander looking for sustenance and safety. Such people live often as strangers and aliens separated "from their own past, culture and country, from their neighbors, friends and family, from their deepest self and their God."[19]

American communities are very often communities of persons who are strangers to one another. In every American community there are those strangers who have recently emigrated to this country seeking political refuge and opportunity. There are also those persons who have come to our communities in a job transfer, in hope of finding work, or in retirement. In addition, in every community, there are the poor and marginalized, some of whom are also homeless. What do these people find in your community? In your community of faith?

In the formative writings of our Christian heritage, we learn that the faith community is first of all to be a home. The apostle Paul instructed the early church to

Welcome one another, therefore, just as Christ
has welcomed you, for the glory of God
(Romans 15:7).

The Christian congregation is absolutely unique in that it exists primarily for those that are not members of it. As heirs of Abraham, and disciples of Jesus, the cornerstone of the church's vocation is to share faith by offering the strangers in our midst the hospitality of home. Or, as Henri Nouwen put it, "to convert the *hostis* into a *hospes,* the enemy into a guest and to create the free and fearless space where brotherhood and sisterhood can be formed and fully experienced."[20]

THE ROOTS OF HOSPITALITY

Our Judeo-Christian understanding of hospitality is rooted in the biblical story of creation and redemption and in the theological legacy of that story. The biblical story begins in a settled and fertile place, actually in a garden, in which the Lord God, "Yahweh," offered the first human beings all the amenities of home. Christian hospitality has its source and center in the heart of God and the creation of God. God's hospitality is evident in the sheer abundance and generosity of God's creation in field and forest, sky and water, and in the connectedness and companionship of all of God's creatures.

---

[19] Henri J.M. Nouwen. *Reaching Out,* (Garden City, NY: Doubleday and Company, 1975), p. 46.
[20] Ibid, p. 46.

As the story is told, Adam and Eve were "at home" in Eden. They were content and at rest, at least initially. They had everything they needed. They had safety, shelter, and ample food in the prolific vegetation in the garden. They also had one another and the companionship of a diverse animal kingdom. In short, they had paradise!

Thus, the Genesis story traces the origin of hospitality back beyond the experience of desert peoples to the generosity of God in creation.

At the same time, the Genesis story traces the origin of the universal human experience of never being fully at home anywhere in the world! Hardly does the story begin before Eden has become "paradise lost," with the first family evicted from the Garden. We remember the story. The Landlord was neither fickle nor evil. On the contrary, the Landlord provided everything for the tenants to live a full and abundant life in the Garden. The first human beings, however, wanted more than what God had provided. For one thing, they wanted to know everything God knew, to be like God. Their wants led them to act contrary to God's command. As a consequence they were forced to live henceforth by their own wit and work rather than by the provision of a benevolent Lord. In the same way they had to find a place for themselves to call home, the home provided for them being no longer available.

Though part of God's creation, we human beings have always been "in but not of the world." We are in it as a part of the created order, but we have always longed for something more, beyond our immediate grasp. "Thou hast made us for thyself," prayed Augustine, "and our hearts are restless until they rest in thee."[21] In the stories we tell, the songs we sing, the art we create, we find witnesses to a deep loneliness in the human soul.

Human beings are driven to find some place "east of Eden" in which they will feel at home. Ever since Cain and Abel, however, the quest for home has often been at the expense of weaker peoples who have been killed or driven from their ancestral lands. History is one long record of how God's gracious hospitality in the Garden has been ignored in subsequent generations.

The place that we human beings are looking for is in the great and generous heart of God revealed and broken in Jesus Christ. To come home to God through faith in Jesus Christ is to come home to Eden. It is "paradise regained!" It is to come home to the reign of God, home from our prodigal wandering, home to the house and rule of our Creator and Redeemer, where all are welcomed and received as members of God's family. Such a homecoming is eschatological, in the sense of being our future and our destiny. It is also realized eschatology, in the sense that in the hospitality of a congregation we can experience a foretaste of

---

[21] Augustine of Hippo, North Africa, 4th Century. *The United Methodist Hymnal* (Nashville: The United Methodist Publishing House, 1989). p. 423.

God's hospitality as created life will eventually give way to God's gift of resurrection.

As human beings and as members of God's covenant community, the church of Jesus Christ, we know that "'a wandering Aramean was [our] ancestor'" (Deuteronomy 26:5). We have been both resident and alien, both the beneficiary of extraordinary hospitality and called to offer this hospitality to others.

In this light, consider again the story of Abraham and Sarah. They offered their guests not only food and shelter, but the very best the couple had to give. They went far beyond the bare necessities. Like visitors today who discover the congregation that genuinely welcomes them, those visitors must have been delighted by the welcome:

> *And Abraham hastened into the tent to Sarah, and said, "Make ready quickly three measures of choice flour, knead it, and make cakes." Abraham ran to the herd, and took a calf, tender and good, and gave it to the servant, who hastened to prepare it. Then he took curds and milk and the calf that he had prepared, and set it before them*
> (Genesis 18:6-8).

Abraham and Sarah offered their very best. Not a little bread but cake made of "choice flour." And not some stringy goat, which desert nomads would have had in ample supply, but a "calf, tender and good!" Beef at its best, and for dessert, "curds and milk." Yogurt!

Such acts of hospitality are just as important today. Consider the story of one woman during the Great Depression. During those years many people fed only the leftovers to strangers, and usually outside the house. This woman, however, always made a special meal and fed her visitors in her kitchen. True hospitality is the offer of all the amenities of home and more. Not a stable out back but the front bedroom! The best seats! The first cut of the roast! How does your congregation give evidence of offering the best you have to strangers?

WHO IS THE STRANGER?

Many people today feel insecure and they hide or "cocoon" behind locked doors and barred windows. Strangers are regarded with fear, not to be trusted until they can prove themselves to be worthy. Christian people who feel this way might not be impolite to a stranger, particularly on a Sunday morning in church. They might say "good morning," or, as the peace is passed, "Christ be with you." But they would go no further to extend a real welcome, the hospitality of their home and fellowship at their table. The church cannot depend on the culture for our understanding of who the stranger is. Our biblical-theological tradition identifies the stranger in much more positive terms.

The stranger is ourselves.

At some time or another we have all been on the outside looking in. Perhaps, as a youth, we may have been "the new kid on the block." Or later, as adults, we may have moved to another part of our own country that is quite different from where we grew up. We may even have been emigrants to a new country. We know something about the self-consciousness, the anxiety, the fear of being a stranger. So it was with Israel. "[Y]ou know the heart of an alien," reads the Law of God, "for you were aliens in the land of Egypt" (Exodus 23:9). The stranger is ourselves, and thus hospitality offered is simply treating others as we would like to be treated.

The stranger is our neighbor.

Neighbor is an important biblical word that defines how we are to regard strangers. In Leviticus 19, God's people are instructed both to "love your neighbor as yourself" and to " love the alien as yourself."[22] Jesus defined "neighbor" not just as one with whom we share identity of race or nationality, but as one who shows mercy to persons in need, as in the parable of the good Samaritan (Luke 10:25-37). Hospitality is being neighborly in the best sense of that word.

The stranger is a revelation of God.

What is most striking about the possibilities that come with strangers is that they can also be an *epiphany*, a revelation of the divine being and presence. The three travelers who were granted the hospitality of Abraham and Sarah's tent were soon revealed to be messengers of God. They spoke God's promise to their hosts that the Lord "will surely return to you in due season, and your wife Sarah shall have a son" (Genesis 18:10). A similar epiphany occurred to the widow of Zarephath who offered food and shelter to Elijah, a messenger of God through whom she was granted an abundance of oil and meal and the raising of her son from the dead (1 Kings 17:9-24).

The most engaging tale of such a blessing occurs, however, in the closing pages of Luke's Gospel (Luke 24:13-35). This is the story of the two travelers to Emmaus and the Stranger who joined them on the road and at the table. Their hearts were warmed and their eyes were opened to Christ's risen presence. In this story, welcoming a stranger is put on the same level as breaking the

---

[22] Leviticus 19, verses 18 and 34 respectively.

bread and drinking the wine of the Eucharist, the Holy
Communion. For the community that first read Luke's Gospel,
there was an obvious recognition in the text of the sacred meal of
the church: "When he was at the table with them, he took bread,
blessed and broke it, and gave it to them" (Luke 24:30). The two
who traveled to Emmaus recognized Christ in the breaking of the
bread, but this moment of recognition was itself dependent on
their former act of hospitality. They were the ones who had urged
the Stranger, "'Stay with us, because it is almost evening and the
day is now nearly over'" (Luke 24:29).

Luke's early readers would have recognized the invitation as
part of the sacramental meal that came later. The travelers invited
a stranger to sit and eat with them. In so doing they met Christ.
Notice that the divine presence was recognized after the dual
offer: hospitality and the breaking of the bread (Luke 24: 29-30). It
was then, Luke tells us, that "their eyes were opened, and they
recognized him" (Luke 24:31). The same dynamic is also evident
in the parable of the Last Judgment (Matthew 25) where Christ is
revealed to those who have practiced hospitality to strangers,
prisoners, and others on the margins of life.

Hospitality is an offer of home. It blesses both the stranger
and the host with new life, shelter, sustenance, and the promise
of a future.

HOSPITALITY IN THE NEW TESTAMENT CHURCH

The New Testament church assumed that all social and cultural distinctions that formally regulated behavior no longer
applied. The church was a colony of heaven and as such modeled
what the reign of God is and would be like. When God reigns
supreme, no one is a stranger. Men and women, said Jesus, "'will
come from east and west and will eat with Abraham and Isaac
and Jacob in the kingdom of heaven'" (Matthew 8:11).

In the two meals at which Jesus served as host, namely the
feeding of the five thousand and the Last Supper, no one was
turned away—neither those who had forgotten to bring their
own supper nor the betrayer. All were welcome and fed, as all
are welcome in God's kingdom through grace and forgiveness.
"'Come to me ,'" says Jesus, to all who are "'weary and are carrying heavy burdens'" (Matthew 11:28). There are no distinctions.
In the same way, the Son of Man will welcome those who offered
hospitality to the stranger, the sick, the imprisoned, the hungry
and homeless (Matthew 25:31-40).

Jesus' vision of the church necessitated the practice of hospitality on the part of his followers. Indeed, it was his gracious welcome to strangers that enabled an international, interracial, class-
less community to come into being, in which "[t]here is no longer

Jew or Greek, there is no longer slave or free, there is no longer male or female" (Galatians 3:28).

Christians in New Testament times were regularly being exhorted to "extend hospitality to strangers" (Romans 12:13). For by doing that, they are reminded, "some have entertained angels without knowing it" (Hebrews 13:2). This statement not only recalls the hospitality of Abraham and Sarah, but also the Emmaus travelers, as well as Jesus' teaching in Matthew 25:31-40. With all the scholastic controversy that often surrounds the biblical text, no one has ever questioned the fact that the New Testament church was a welcoming church.

In the first really systematic treatise of Christian theology and ethics, Paul's letter to the church at Rome, hospitality seems to rank as highly on the ethical side as justification and life in the Spirit do on the theological side. Christians, Paul wrote, should not just please themselves, but instead "[e]ach of us must please our neighbor for the good purpose of building up the neighbor" (Romans 15:2). Such pleasing of the neighbor will issue in tolerance toward those Paul describes as "weak in faith," those who as a support to their faith follow the strict dietary laws they had learned from Judaism. "If your brother or sister is being injured by what you eat," Paul reminds the stronger members of the community, "you are no longer walking in love" (Romans 14:15).

Paramount in the strategy of being a faith-sharing congregation is the practice of biblical hospitality.

DIMENSIONS OF HOSPITALITY

Any discussion on hospitality needs to take into consideration the welcome and inclusion of persons in worship, in fellowship, and also in opportunities to "do" ministry.

People need to be needed. If they cannot participate in meaningful work they will not be completely welcomed into the congregation. Many congregations make a serious error in leaving new members alone, believing the newcomers need time to get acquainted before they are given a job to do. The reality is quite the opposite. There is some evidence that after the first year of membership, as many as half of the new members in mainline congregations are either inactive or well on the way. Much of the reason for such a statistic is the failure to extend hospitality beyond the act of joining the congregation. People get acquainted and make friends and learn by doing common tasks. Strangers not only receive the gifts of hospitality, but they come offering the gift of a different future, if in fact they are invited to serve God's reign through the congregation.

A case in point is the coming of a new pastor to a congregation. Studies of congregations over several years have noted major changes in such fundamental statistics as worship attendance and giving. More often than not, such statistical upcurves are related to a new pastor or other staff person. Yet, in some congregations, that same increase in kingdom activity has followed the coming of a new lay person who responds to an invitation to offer his or her gifts in and through that local congregation. In a congregation in northern New Jersey, an acquaintance of one of the authors was received into a new congregation with genuine hospitality. The result was a small group ministry in that congregation, as well as the introduction of the Walk to Emmaus ministry in that region.[23] This was made possible all because she was invited to offer the gift of her own needs, interests, and life experience.

What is true for new members is also true for long-standing members. Consider the story of a couple we will call John and Mary. John and Mary were charter members of a mainline congregation in a New York suburb. In their early years of membership, with three children at home, they had been extremely busy in the congregation. As years went by they aged and slowed down. They were asked to do fewer and fewer tasks. They stopped attending as regularly as they used to. When asked why this was so, John answered, "It doesn't feel like we are needed anymore; we never get asked to do anything!"

The scope of a congregation's hospitality is also informed by the quality of care and relationship it offers to strangers. In the Genesis account of Abraham and Sarah, *the couple offered the best they had to offer.* To offer the best in a local congregation means, among other things, that a congregation's hospitality should not be sidelined to a small committee's responsibility. Hospitality is not a task to be assigned to a committee. It is not maintenance but ministry, and thus the work of the whole church. Hospitality that is biblically informed and guided is not a public relations strategy to encourage church growth but a congregational lifestyle, chosen in order to be obedient to God's vision for the church. It demands center stage in the practice of the local congregation.

How do members of a congregation learn to make small acts of sacrifice a way of life? What small acts of sacrifice does your congregation have to offer? Some congregations encourage members to pass up the most convenient parking spaces, reserving them for visitors. Practicing habits of sacrifice can take many forms.

Consider the story of Edna in a midwestern city. All her life she had tried to fulfill other people's expectations. In later life, after a divorce and a move to another city, she began to attend church again. In this new church, she had her own identity. On her first

---

[23] The Walk to Emmaus is a 72-hour Christian formation experience that is usually held at a retreat center. It is a Protestant expression of the Roman Catholic "cursillo." For further information, write to The Upper Room Walk to Emmaus, P.O. Box 340004, Nashville, TN 37203-0004 (www.upperroom.org/emmaus).

Sunday she was greeted by a woman sitting next to her, who invited her to share lunch together after worship. During the meal, her new friend told her story and the role that congregation played in it. That week Edna received an invitation to a small group meeting of women who were all on a spiritual journey of discovery of self and God. Later, Edna responded to a pulpit announcement about the availability of a care ministry to people in need. She called the care center about a friend she had been trying to help. A contact was made that same day. Edna was delighted with the swiftness and quality of the response to her friend's need and is today a serving lay minister within the same care ministry. She has learned, through hospitality, who she is. She is Edna, a child of God.

WELCOMING, BELONGING, AND DISCIPLING.

Hospitality, if it is only a casual greeting on a Sunday morning from an official greeter, is far less than Abraham and Sarah offered. There is so much more. Hospitality is part of the primary task or core process of all the local congregation. It describes the quality of the welcome, and the openness of the congregation to new persons. Leonard Sweet has coined the phrase, "hospitality evangelism." He understands that faith is shared by a congregation's lifestyle of hospitality more profoundly than by many of the favored methodologies of traditional personal evangelism. Hospitality evangelism, in Sweet's analysis, has three aspects to it: invitation, introduction, and initiation.[24]

Hospitality is not an end in itself, but part of an "evangelical flow" as persons move through the congregation to their citizenship in the reign of God. The goal of the church is God's kingdom on earth as in heaven. The congregation's primary task is related to that goal and includes reaching out to people, receiving them into fellowship, providing opportunities for them to grow in their relationship with God, nurturing them in faith, and sending them out to serve the ends of the kingdom in the places where God appoints. The role of hospitality is to create an environment in which this evangelical flow moves without barriers or constraints.

Put another way, this evangelical flow can be expressed in three movements:

WELCOMING MINISTRIES
in which the stranger is reached out to and received as an honored guest,

---

[24] Leonard Sweet. *Quantum Spirituality: A Postmodern Apologetic.* (Dayton, Ohio: Whaleprints, 1991), pp. 198-213.

BELONGING MINISTRIES
in which the guest is incorporated into the community and
becomes a member of the church family,

and

DISCIPLING MINISTRIES
in which the new member, through teaching, prayer, fellowship, and service, is taught and incorporated into the reign of
God and sent out to serve.

These three movements within the evangelical flow form
another way to describe the primary system of a congregation.
Remember the discussion about the primary task? The primary
task is a system in which people enter and are welcomed. They
participate in various settings that help them pursue their spiritual journey. The desired result of such a system is Christian disciples who are aware of their own gifts and call to ministry. They
leave the congregation settings behind to live their lives in family,
neighborhood, and work place. In those settings they work to
make the community more loving and just, as well as to invite
people to return with them to the faith community. This is a
statement of the primary task in functional language. To speak of
welcoming, belonging, and discipling is the same primary task
more in the language of spiritual formation. We find it helpful to
represent this model not only as an evangelical flow, but also as a
spiritual spiral.

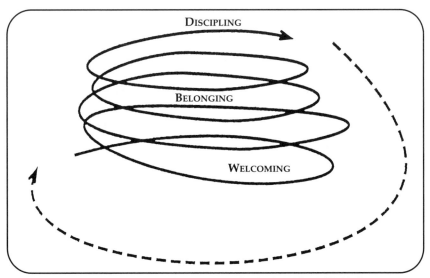

Quest for Quality, A New Way of Thinking Notebook. (Nashville: General Board of Discipleship)

Paul wrote to the Ephesians that "we must grow up in every way into him who is the head, into Christ" (4:15).

WELCOMING

Welcoming is the offer of friendship. It is an invitation to come to Christ by coming into the Christian community. In regard to the stranger, this period of welcoming may last only for a few weeks or it may extend much longer, depending on the needs of the person seeking welcome.

It would be a serious error, however, to think of "welcoming ministries" as related only to newcomers. People are always in transition. They often need to be re-welcomed as circumstances in life change.

Consider the story of Henry and Helen. They had been "pillars" in their local congregation. Much of their participation was as a couple. They team-taught a Sunday school class, sang in the choir together, and served on the congregation's governing board together. When Helen died, Henry was understandably lonely. As he later told his pastor, it seemed to him that he wasn't the same person anymore.

And, indeed, he was not. He didn't feel like a member any more, he said, partly because so much of the church's activity kept reminding him of his loss. Henry needed to be reached and received all over again in a welcoming ministry that offered the new Henry blessings of Christian friendship as warm and genuine as those he and his wife had enjoyed together.

Who are some of the persons who need to be re-welcomed into your congregation? What about the youth who have grown up in a congregation, gone off to college elsewhere, then returned to the church of their youth, only to become inactive? The congregation assumed that they were already incorporated because they had once been. Congregations also change as the membership changes and new leaders come. The challenge in welcoming ministries is to keep the church door open as wide as possible. The next chapter will offer practical examples of welcoming ministries.

BELONGING

The process of moving into the fellowship circle of the congregation, or *belonging*, may be a brief or extended period. We will say more about the time frame for belonging in the next chapter. For now, let us look at a simple definition of what it means to belong to a congregation. It means more, of course, than membership. Membership in the congregation for many is little more than being on a list. Many persons join a congregation before they really belong to it.

Belonging has to do with believing. Real belonging is related to the apostolic experience of *kerygma,* of taking the Christian message to heart. Belonging has to do with believing the central core of Christian faith, as expressed in that familiar greeting and benediction of the church, the "grace of the Lord Jesus Christ, the love of God, and the communion of the Holy Spirit" (2 Corinthians 13:13). Real belonging involves being related to God and nurtured in faith. It includes personal appropriation and ownership of Christian faith. It includes identification with the beliefs and value system of a congregation, as well as with its mission and ministry goals.

There is a crisis today in membership growth in all of the mainline Protestant denominations in America. In The United Methodist Church, for instance, as much as half of the congregations in a typical year report not one person received into the congregation on profession of faith. In many a congregation this is the result of indifference rather than of a lack of prospects.

Having said that, growing churches also face the temptation to receive people into membership too casually and often prematurely. What is the rush into membership? Quick decisions to join a congregation may be based on surface impressions or the emotion of the moment, rather than on the weightier issue of the alignment of personal faith with the faith of the congregation. Belonging to a congregation, in the best sense of the phrase, implies a beginning of a journey into discipleship. In the next chapter we will return to this consideration of belonging ministries, and offer some practical examples.

DISCIPLING

The third movement in the evangelical flow is *discipling* or initiating persons into the reign of God. Some Protestants will differentiate between belonging to a congregation and being a disciple of Jesus Christ. Such a distinction is a concession to the reality of nominal membership, but it is unfortunate and non-Wesleyan. It is based not so much on the classic theology of the church as on a long history of inadequate preparation of persons for membership in the congregation. The gospels record that Jesus never turned anyone away from the benefits of his public ministries of healing and teaching. Any and all persons were welcome. Yet he also differentiated between the welcoming of persons and the more intense challenge of discipleship.

Discipleship was costly! Discipleship meant following Jesus and making a complete change in priorities. It also involved a lifestyle characterized by simplicity and service. "'None of you,'" Luke records Jesus as saying, "'can become my disciple if you do not give up all your possessions'" (Luke 14:33). In this same passage Jesus counseled careful consideration before making a decision:

"'which of you, intending to build a tower, does not first sit down and estimate the cost, to see whether he has enough to complete it?'" (Luke 14: 28). Was Jesus being less gracious in his invitation to discipleship than he was in his invitation to those carrying heavy burdens? "'Come to me'" (Matt. 11:28). We think not. He was telling it like it is.

To belong to the congregation, to be incorporated into the *corpus,* the body of Christ, is a gracious invitation to come to Christ and to follow Christ. It also involves using one's gifts for ministry. We do a disservice if we do not prepare people adequately for discipleship. This includes a thorough orientation to the Christian *kerygma,* the ethics of the reign of God, and both the mission and the ministry of the local congregation. The meaning of membership needs to be raised to the level of discipleship, not lowered from it. For practical examples of discipling ministries, see the next chapter.

SUMMARY

Hospitality in the faith-sharing congregation extends through the whole process of welcoming, belonging, and discipling. Therefore the concern for and issue of hospitality will not end at some future time when the person is supposed to be fully incorporated. Hospitality, to be effective, must be more than a program. It must be a congregational lifestyle. It must be part of the total environment of the congregation.

Hospitality is not church work, but the work of the church. It is not maintenance of the institution but ministry in Jesus' name. It is the experience of being at home with God's family, the congregation. It includes the initial welcome of the newcomer and follows through with the goal of incorporating and initiating that person into the service of God.

The goal of hospitality is wonderfully expressed in lines from Isaac Watts, that each person, in God's House will be:

No more a stranger, nor a guest, but like a child at home.[25]

---

[25] Isaac Watts, "My Shepherd Will Supply My Need." (Minneapolis: Art Master Studio Inc.).

3

Ministries of Welcoming Belonging, and Discipling

Modern households usually include two small instruments that resemble one another in appearance. They are actually very different in their functions. One is a thermometer, the other a thermostat.

The thermometer simply displays the temperature. The thermostat, however, has the capacity to make a difference by responding to the need. It slowly and steadily changes the climate by turning on the furnace or the air conditioner, depending on which is needed.

In the life of local congregations, hospitality ministries resemble the thermostat. No other program emphasis has as much potential for making a difference as hospitality. Yet, as we have seen, hospitality is not a subheading under ministry. Hospitality is a climate of inclusiveness. It is people-centered, not program-centered. It is a way of being the church. It is the church practicing what it preaches. It is how congregations share their faith in God's great generosity revealed in Jesus.

Stories abound of the hospitality of congregations that have had the climate that encourages new birth. One such story is of two brothers, unchurched and growing up on the streets of a city in the northeastern United States. They made it a practice to break into a church in their neighborhood, not to do vandalism but to seek refuge from summer's heat and winter's cold. One day they were caught by the pastor. They expected the pastor to call the police; instead he offered them a key to the building. The neighborhood, he noticed, teemed with children and teenagers. Very few came to the traditional Sunday school that was offered. Like Abraham, with the strangers who came to his tent, the pastor offered the young men all the comforts of home. "Of all the people in this neighborhood," he said to them, "you are trying the hardest to get into this church." A room was offered for a boys' club, which became, months later, a Sunday school class. Not long after that, the boys' class and a girls' class merged into a youth fellowship. Two of those youth later went into the ordained ministry. Several others became active lay workers in other congregations.

The following illustrate a variety of ministries showing hospitality within the three categories of welcoming, belonging, and discipling. This is not meant to be an exhaustive list of all possibilities. Under each classification you will find one or more issues close to what is primary and basic in hospitality. Attention at these critical points will change the climate in the congregation as a whole.

I. WELCOMING MINISTRIES
A. THE MINISTRY OF SPACE

Many of us have been trying for a long time to correct the popular assumption that a church is a building. Yes, "the church is a people!" We must not forget, however, how important a church building is. Buildings, like people, can either be warm and welcoming or cold and forbidding.

To create space for a congregation to live in can be a challenging adventure. There are often community restrictions to deal with and sometimes conflict within the congregation as to what a church should look like. "It doesn't look like a church!" Those words have been heard at more than one building committee meeting. "When I die," a friend who is a pastor once wrote on completing a building project, "if I wake up in a building committee meeting, I'll know where I am, and it won't be heaven!" For him, however, as for many pastors and lay leaders, the effort can be very satisfying when it results in a space that is sacramental, in space that conveys the graciousness and generosity of God's welcome in Jesus Christ. (A good architect also helps!)

Most of us, however, have to live with buildings bequeathed to us by earlier generations. A creative architect can help in this situation as well. Yet there are things the rest of us can do to make our buildings truly hospitable to people.

First, we can make them as appealing as possible. Something as simple as investing in lawn care or a few gallons of paint can send a powerful message. As we said before, how the message comes to us has as much to do with whether and how the message is heard as does the content of the message itself. A carefully constructed sermon delivered by an unkempt preacher standing amid the clutter of misplaced hymnals and accumulations of old Sunday school papers, used bulletins, and withered flowers, would not be nearly as absorbing or appreciated as it would be if preached by someone well-groomed and in an appealing setting. The "care and feeding" of church property for the sake of being welcoming is one instance when maintenance can be ministry.

One senior pastor, whenever there is a staff addition, requests the new person to spend the first week on the job evaluating the physical facility. The assumption behind such an assignment is that new staff persons, like new members, bring "new eyes" that notice things others no longer see.

Consider, on a yearly basis, a re-evaluation of the physical space. Is it as attractive and as useful as it can be? Are there barriers to the entry of persons with disabling conditions? Are there barriers to people being able to see and feel close to one another? Is there also a sense of closeness to God? Is the worship space inspiring? Seasonal banners on the walls call people to prepare for worship. Sometimes very simple changes convey a whole world of meanings.

A growing congregation in the northeast, housed in a Victorian-age structure, has eliminated pulpit and lectern. Now, at the center of the once pulpit-centered sanctuary, is a table, covered with a special quilt. The pastor stands at the table or behind it. There are no barriers between pastor and people. The church feels open and conveys a sense of being open to God as well.

Special attention should be given to signs. Can people find their way to your church from, say, six blocks away? When they get there, can they find the sanctuary, the pastor's study, the rest rooms, the nursery? Long-time members know where everything is and can easily forget that new people do not.

What does your church sign say? Does it carry a message of welcome in some other way than the typical "Visitors Welcome?" Such an invitation might lead people to expect more than the congregation is willing to offer. A friend took a year off from serving on a church staff and decided to "shop around" for a congregation to attend. A small country church had attracted her whenever she drove by. She noticed that the Sunday service of worship was at 10 o'clock in the morning. The next Sunday, at five minutes before the hour, she entered to find the congregation well into the service. Later, she learned that the service had started at 9:30. When she pointed out the error on the outside sign, the remark was made that people no longer paid attention to that sign: "Everybody who needed to know about the change had been told."

Another ministry of space is to offer the use of your church to the community. In every community there are ministries, in the broadest sense of that word, who have no office or meeting space of their own, but must depend on public space such as schools and churches. There are also a number of "for profit" groups looking for inexpensive space for exercise and diet programs. Should a church use its facilities to buoy up a battered budget? It is an important policy decision for the church to consider.[26] One congregation has stipulated that every use of its building must "honor and offer Christ." Others allow no use of the buildings except by non-profit groups that serve the needs of people in the community. In this category may be continuing education courses, Red Cross blood drives, or support groups for people in recovery from addictions to alcohol, tobacco, and other drugs.

An issue in regard to such groups is how to best practice hospitality. Most congregations provide authorized persons with keys to the building and leave it at that. One congregation has instituted a church host program. Each evening, Monday through Friday, a host is assigned to be on the premises. Duties of the host include unlocking the premises, greeting persons using the building, giving directions to church facilities, and being generally as helpful and as hospitable as possible.

Hosts have opportunities to answer questions about the church and its ministries. Occasionally, upon invitation, the pastor in this congregation makes brief visits to the groups to extend a personal welcome. The result has been a number of unexpected persons seeking out other services the church has to offer.

B. Hospitality to Children

"Our children," writes Henri Nouwen, "are our most important guests."[27] The practice of infant baptism by many mainline denominations points to the central place children occupy in the life of the congregation. Children belong in church. In baptism, we affirm that children are not the private property of the family, nor are they the community's property. They are a gift, given from God to enrich both church and family. Yet, sadly, in many congregations ministry to children occurs on the periphery of the congregation's life.

A new pastor in a west Texas congregation was invited by the church's lay leader to a personal tour of the community. The pastor learned later that the other man was a retired rancher and had a terminal illness. At the close of a half-day of driving around the county, the lay leader parked in front of the parsonage. "I have

---

[26] Allowing "for profit" groups to use church facilities has a number of insurance and tax implications. Congregations are advised to investigate local and state law, as well as tax law for "non-profit" institutions before agreeing to such usage.

[27] Henri J.M. Nouwen. *Reaching Out* (Garden City: Doubleday and Company, 1975), p. 56.

one dream," he said to his pastor. "Before I die I am hoping to see children in our church again."

A check of the facts showed that indeed the church's ministry to children had been in serious decline for many years. The children's division of the Sunday school was small, and children were rarely in the church service. "What would it take for the congregation to become hospitable to children?" was the question the pastor asked himself. That should be every congregation's question. What changes can your congregation make so that children feel at home? What is the price of hospitality to children?

This particular pastor began to act as if children were already there in the service. Each Sunday the congregation sang a hymn that children would have enjoyed singing. Worship was planned with children in mind, with more movement and music added, and with storytelling as a major part of the sermon. There was no children's sermon as such, but in addition to preaching with stories, the pastor worked hard at telling the gospel in simple ways a child could understand.

An encouraging result came one Sunday morning when the organist leaned over to the pastor during the service. "If you keep this up," she said, "I'll have to bring my grandchildren to church." She did and others did too. Before the lay leader died, most of the congregation's children were back where they belonged.

Consider what it might mean in your congregation to declare "a year of the child." Remember that a new year for the church begins not with the calendar year, but with Advent. Children easily feel at home when they can think and talk and sing about Christmas and the wonderful way God reached out to us in a Child.

Begin with worship. First, be sure that children are able to attend the worship service. Unfortunately, an increasing number of congregations are scheduling Sunday school at the same hour as worship. The message is clear: children don't belong in the sanctuary. Beyond changing that message, how can you make worship attractive to children? It does not have to be childish or distracting to adults. The service needs to keep moving so as to respect the attention span of children. (Adults will appreciate this, too.) Preaching that includes occasional drama or visual aids such as a short clip from a videotape will engage children with the gospel.

Some other issues around hospitality to children include space and safety. Are the rooms for children's ministries the best they can be? People with artistic gifts can add interest to a room. In New Mexico a congregation has created a Noah's Ark decor for the Sunday school area. Clean toys and cribs are important to parents leaving children in a nursery or toddler room. Are the children themselves aware of such things? We think so! A clean environment is a factor in a positive experience for all ages.

Are small children safe in your Sunday school and church? Some churches have a simple sign-in and sign-out sheet. The same person who signs the child in must also sign the child out. A number system also works. Pin a number on a child's clothing that corresponds to a number the parent is given. Numbers must match before a child is released into an adult's charge. Simple things to remember that extend hospitality to small children and their parents include:

1. Always have at least two teachers in a classroom, no matter how small the class.
2. Screen your teachers and know them well before you put them in charge of children.
3. Keep your rooms bright, cheerful, and clean.
4. Consider whether or not drinking fountains, coatracks, and bathrooms are "child-friendly."
5. Train your teachers in safety and hospitality as well as skills in using curriculum.[28]

Hospitality to children will demand the best we have to give in terms of time and energy, imagination, and creativity. "The present crisis of evangelism," argues Walter Brueggemann, in *Biblical Perspectives on Evangelism*, "is in great measure because the community of the church has not persuaded our own young of the power or validity of the gospel." This has happened, he continues, largely because "adults have been inarticulate within the family of faith about our faith."[29]

C. THE MINISTRY OF INVITATION

A North Carolina lay preacher gave his definition of church. "The church," he said, "is what you have left over when the building burns down and the preacher leaves town." The church is more than a place, or any one person. The church is people, the people of God, the *laos*.

But church is something else as well. It is a *happening*. Something happens when the people of God meet. God meets with them. Souls are stirred. Singing, storytelling, the sacraments are all ways to meet the needs of individuals as varied and diverse as the number of persons present. One person may find a sense of healing or order that has been missing in life. Another may wish to receive baptism or to begin the process of belonging

---

[28] For additional resources, see *Safe Sanctuaries: Reducing the Risk of Child Abuse in the Church* (Discipleship Resources, 800-972-0433 or www.discipleshipresources.org), *Reducing the Risk of Child Sexual Abuse Prevention Kit* (Christian Ministry Resources, P.O. Box 2301, Matthews, NC 28106), and video *Hear Their Cries: Religious Responses to Child Abuse* (Center for Prevention of Sexual and Domestic Violence, 2400 N. 45th St. #10, Seattle, WA 98103).

[29] Walter Brueggemann, *Biblical Perspectives on Evangelism: Living in a Three-Storied Universe* (Nashville: Abingdon Press, 1993), p. 126.

to the congregation. A couple may wish to pray for their marriage. Someone may hear God's call to a volunteer task, or to the ordained or diaconal ministry. As at all times when God has been present in power, people's lives are changed.

Consider the story of Bob, a successful businessman, who carried deep wounds that had never healed from experiences with the church as a child. Except for rare and ceremonial occasions, his wife and family attended without him. One Sunday a granddaughter persuaded him to come to hear her sing. Watching her sing with her friends, Bob was deeply touched. Was it the innocent joy of his granddaughter and her friends? Was it their childlike trust in God? Whatever it was, Bob found himself in a place where he had never been before: on the edge of profound conviction and surrender.

Fortunately, the morning's service contained an invitation to which persons, including Bob, could respond. To offer an invitation for people to act on their need is a profound ministry of hospitality to persons. It enables a person to relate to God. Many pastors and congregations are apprehensive about offering an invitation for fear of seeming manipulative. They fail to see that to withhold the opportunity for persons to respond to the gospel could also be manipulative.

In the church Bob's family attended, every Sunday just before the benediction the pastor offered a special invitation. "Church isn't just an hour," Bob heard him say. "Church is an opportunity to praise God and to pray to God and to find your needs met. If church isn't over for you this morning, you are invited to remain in this sanctuary following the benediction. You are invited to come and use the communion rail as a place for prayer. If you wish, someone will meet with you and pray with you. You may stay as long as you want. Those of you for whom church is over are asked to leave the sanctuary quietly." Bob whispered to his wife that he would meet her outside. He made his way toward the front of the sanctuary, sat in the first pew, and prayed. Today Bob is a witness to the generosity of God's love in Jesus Christ.

But what if the invitation had not been given? Fortunately, the worship leader recognized that the church's hospitality was increased through an invitation for people to allow God's Spirit to communicate with their spirits.

The hope and promise is that whenever God's people meet in worship, "church" will happen. Do we provide in our liturgies and worship experiences a time and a place for God to minister directly with people? And when we do, do we constrict the Spirit by offering only one type of invitation, such as joining the church, or making a first-time commitment to Christ? To allow time for the invitation to remain open is to practice profound hospitality.

Some congregations have Holy Communion available following every service. This practice addresses the many needs that people have, including the need to remain in God's presence for a longer period than the corporate worship service provides.

Invitations can come in many forms. In one service, after a sermon on sensitivity between generations, the pastor asked those present, if they felt comfortable doing so, to seek out someone in the congregation from another generation. They were asked to pray together, or just to greet one another and visit for a few moments. A woman turned around, looking for an older woman, found herself face to face with a teenage girl. They greeted one another. Suddenly the girl began to cry and leaned against the woman. A conversation followed, then a midweek phone call. A simple invitation to respond to the message opened up a new possibility of ministry.

II. BELONGING MINISTRIES
A. MAKING MEMBERSHIP MEANINGFUL

Incorporation into the body of Christ involves a public act or ritual of joining. Persons are formally introduced and offered "the hand of fellowship."[30] It is a step in the journey of discipleship, to bond with a people of God for mutual support and ministry. However, as many have observed, the decision to join a church is often followed by a period of testing, after which another less formal but important decision is made. That decision is whether to become an increasingly active member or to explore other possibilities. A critical juncture comes at the point of the person's deciding whether or not to take on a role in the congregation.

➤➤ Decision to	➤➤ Period of	➤➤ Decision to
join a church	testing, learning the ropes.	participate taking on a role in church, or not.

Used by permission of Discipleship Resources, Nashville, TN

It is not uncommon for persons to join a congregation and later decide to sever the relationship or, more likely, to render it void by becoming a marginal member.

The "system" of how American Protestants join a church probably encourages the results we are getting. As many as one half of the adults who join mainline churches drop into inactivity in their first year of membership. A new system is needed. Such a system would not invite persons to prematurely join a congregation but to enter into a period of association. During that time

---

[30] Baptismal Covenant III, *The United Methodist Hymnal* (Nashville: United Methodist Publishing House, 1989). p. 48.

persons could test whether they and the congregation of their choice are a good match. The congregation would provide settings for people to explore their yearnings for God and to continue on their spiritual journey. To have a fellowship friend or sponsor available for friendship and counsel would be beneficial.

A process of incorporation is needed in which persons are first invited to meet with a small group of other newcomers. Together they could ponder the considerations involved in a decision for membership. Finally, those ready to become members of the family would be received in a ceremony that gives stature and dignity to church membership, rather than being inserted at the end of the service like an afterthought.

The value of such a system is that it releases anxiety about having to make a decision quickly. It also forms a natural small group that can have lasting influence on each person's growth in discipleship. Finally, it makes membership in the church an act of affirmation of faith as well as an occasion of joy.

Depending on the size of the congregation, groups for "membership inquiry" can be set up monthly, quarterly, or every six months. A clear invitation is given to consider whether membership in this congregation is right at the present time. Even in a congregation with small membership such groups are possible. A group of two or three persons is still better than trying to do membership training one-on-one. In a small group the newcomer is offered the dual opportunity to inquire about membership and to bond with another person or persons. Those who fail to bond with someone else within the congregation will probably be less likely to become active members.

In one congregation, the membership inquiry group meets for the first time following the worship service on a Sunday morning. Luncheon is served. There is an invitation to explore the meaning of membership. Then group members spend some time getting to know one another. Because this is a larger membership congregation, the early afternoon session closes with a tour of the buildings.

This first meeting is followed by four other meetings, with time available for staff and new persons to get to know each other. At this time persons are encouraged to share their faith journeys with one another. Careful presentations are given about basic Christian beliefs and about what is unique in the doctrinal heritage of the denomination. Selected members of the congregation share the mission and ministry goals of the church and the central role of the laity in the church's ministry. Members are invited to consider where and how they might offer their gifts to God in the life of the congregation. On the last evening session, the lay leader and the pastor share their vision of God's future for the congregation. The evening concludes with a celebration of the Holy Communion.

A service of reception is held two weeks later. This reception takes place at the mid-point of the worship service that the person has usually attended. Prior to this day each group member has been personally contacted and counseled about whether a readiness for membership is there at that particular time.

Making membership as meaningful as possible is a genuine act of hospitality to persons, allowing them to move at their own pace in making such an important decision. All persons need time to reflect on their own gifts, and when and how to use them in ministry to others.

When has such an inquiry group completed its unique life together? Group members might be invited to consider staying together as a group within the church, to meet together regularly for fellowship, study, and prayer. A number of groups in the congregation could be constituted in this way and lasting friendships could be made.

B. GETTING DROPOUTS TO DROP BACK IN,

Picture a mother, a father, and their little girl on vacation in a provincial park in Canada. Hand in hand, the girl and her mother walked the short distance between the campsite and the rest room. They did not return to their campsite together, however. The little girl had told her mother that she knew the way back. She didn't! Within minutes the father and mother moved from anger to terror. No effort was spared. Other campers joined the search. The girl was found.

In your congregation what do you think the result would be if you and congregation members felt the same anxiety and exerted the same effort when, through inactivity, a member becomes lost to the church family? Sometimes it is suggested that inactive people be left to themselves. For time spent, results with such persons, we are told, don't warrant the effort. Working with new prospects will bring quicker and more visible results. Let us remember the parable of the lost sheep. The shepherd has ninety-nine sheep there in the wilderness. Nevertheless, he goes looking for one who is missing (Luke 15: 3-7). The gospel standard is that when one person is not where he or she should be, in God's house and with God's family, we go after that person!

In many mainline congregations, very little or no effort is made to nurture its nonparticipating and indifferent members. Such persons who drift into inactivity are often regarded with hostility and anger as having broken their vows or somehow lost their faith. It is their fault and their responsibility alone to find their way back. Not many do! Most may become victims of an annual attempt to "clean up" the rolls.

Belonging ministries in an inviting congregation should include some system of contact and re-invitation to persons who, for their own reasons, have become marginalized. The system should have at least three components: 1) data gathering, 2) prayer, and 3) a plan.

DATA GATHERING

The first step is to identify those persons who are inactive. Why are they inactive? How many are there? What percentage of the congregation is represented? These are important questions that will get you beyond false assumptions to reality.

Why do people leave congregations? There are any number of reasons. Research by Robert W. Jeambey, reported in the July/August 1993 issue of *Congregations* (published by the Alban Institute), reveals that people who quit churches tend to exhibit a common habit of behavior. They do not feel comfortable in their church relationship. Most people considering such an action will drop out for a test period, sometimes to see if anyone notices. Jeambey's research centers around three primary causes for inactivity.

1. Failed expectations account for 43% of people who become dissatisfied and withdraw.
2. Non-acceptance and unrelatedness account for another 43%. Differences and misunderstandings arise with individuals and groups within the congregation. Friends may have moved away. In general, such persons come to feel as if they are not important to the life of the congregation.
3. Lifestyle conflicts and changes account for 14% of those who become dissatisfied and withdraw. A spouse may have died, or a change of the congregation's worship may have caused dissatisfaction.

We as church leaders too often hold untested assumptions about inactive members. We can carry inward hostility toward inactive members because they are not "pulling their own weight," while we are working "overtime." We suspect that such persons did not unite with the congregation in good faith. The truth is quite the opposite. Studies show that people who become inactive have valid reasons for doing so. Many of them actually do not think of themselves as inactive. Some are practicing the churchmanship that was modeled for them as children, either by their parents or by members of the church at that time in their lives.

PRAYER

As a second step, ask your church leaders and others who assist in the care of members to join in a prayer effort. Rather than praying a general prayer for "all those inactive members," assign the names of one or two to each church leader or committee member. Ask them to pray daily for the person or persons whose names have been assigned to them. Suggest a definite time when this commitment will have been met. Do not allow the effort gradually to be forgotten. Suggest that your leaders ask for blessings for those persons for whom they pray, as well as an opportunity to communicate. Prayer should help your leaders raise their consciousness about specific persons who are precious and valued in God's sight.

A PLAN

Finally, develop a feasible plan that can be tested, adjusted, and worked. That plan ought to include several face-to-face conversations with persons who have become inactive. Communication is the key. Personal contact when someone is first showing signs of dissatisfaction is the best preventive strategy of all. As a general rule, no person should be absent for three consecutive Sundays without being contacted. In congregations with smaller memberships, everyone knows who is missing on any given Sunday morning. In larger congregations attendance registration proves effective for discovering the same information. Computer programs are available that "flag" which persons have been absent for a significant time period. Most inactive members need and want to be courted again. They need and want to know that the congregation esteems them.

Such a plan may include special campaigns at Christmas and/or Lent and Easter to come "home for the holidays," with personal invitations offered to everyone. When persons do return, it is important that they receive recognition. Avoid embarrassing them by calling public attention to their presence. A personal note from the pastor or a church leader, then a follow-up visit, will center attention on the importance of persons, and show respect for their feelings about belonging and about themselves as active or inactive.

III. Discipling Ministries
A. Gifts for Ministry

The heart of discipleship is service. In the process of welcoming, faith is explored and tested; through belonging ministries, we build a church family with whom we can live out the faith we profess. Discipling is different from welcoming. Though it begins with being welcomed and incorporated into a congregation, discipleship has a focus exterior to the self. That focus is Jesus, the reign of God, the pressing needs of people, those around us and those in the world beyond us. No matter how we describe it, discipleship is essentially the sacrificial giving of self through the sharing of those gifts God has given us. "'A disciple,'" said Jesus, "'is not above the teacher'" (Luke 6:40). He spoke of coming "'not to be served but to serve, and to give his life a ransom for many'" (Mark 10:45). On the evening of Easter, the risen Lord said to the gathered disciples, "'As the Father has sent me, so I send you'" (John 20:21). Discipleship is being sent forth to serve with the gifts that God gives for that purpose.

When we allow persons in the congregation, including strangers, to explore and test the gifts for service that God may have given them, we offer them another gift, the gift of hospitality. Hospitality is not just making room for people in our space; it is also accepting the gifts they bring with them to enrich our lives and our communities of faith.

Hospitality also acknowledges that all the baptized are called and gifted for the work of ministry. Indeed, ministry is the work of the whole church, not, as generally practiced, the sole task of the clergy. The unique work and calling of the clergy is leadership. The work of the people is ministry. No discipleship ministry will have greater impact on the whole congregation than the use of the separate gifts that God gives to each individual within that ministry.

Congregations need to do more than listen to an annual Reformation Sunday sermon about the priesthood of all believers. For too long Protestants have talked about the importance of the laity, then acted as clerically autocratic as the pre-Reformation church.

The question is how to move toward a culture of hospitality in which discipleship becomes more than a word. It begins in the hearts of the leadership of the congregation. Effective leaders need to be personally open to receiving ministry from the laity as well as to promoting the concept. The pastor's primary role is to be an "equipping" leader rather than a "doer of my work of ministry with lay help." Clergy ought to exist to help the laity do their ministry.

At Church of the Servant in Oklahoma City, professional staff are expected to make ministry happen, not to do the work of ministry. Annual evaluation and remuneration, they are told, are based on the job they are *not* doing! The job description for professional staff is one of *equipping the laity* for ministry. The staff minister of congregational care, for instance, is not a pastoral counselor offering direct services. Instead, she directs a ministry of congregational care, helping people to discover their gifts for caregiving, equipping them to improve their gifts, providing them with opportunities to do their ministry.

In another congregation the pastor had a vision of a pastoral staff of thirty persons to adequately care for a growing congregation. Three years later there were thirty-two lay ministers of pastoral care in that congregation, called by the congregation, and equipped by the pastor and staff. In this congregation, the members actually nominated persons who fit a profile of a caring, pastoral person.

Most congregations, of course, are not of a size to have a paid staff beyond a pastor and perhaps a part-time secretary. In many small membership congregations, ministry is happening all the time between members. People quite naturally pitch in to help where they are needed. As a result, it may be easier for an imaginative pastor of a small membership congregation to call and equip persons for lay ministry roles than in larger congregations. Often, the presence of a large staff may send a message that ministry is being taken care of by those paid to take care of it.

The ordained leader's challenge is to help individuals recognize their gifts and use them in ministry. An imaginative leader will use the pulpit and lectern to promote the vision of a congregation in which the gifting of the Holy Spirit is recognized and supported. People need to know about their own gifts, which include their life experience, their talents, and their interests. They need to be aware, too, that there are times when God calls someone to a work for which that person may have neither experience nor talent nor even interest. These are the "spiritual gifts" described in 1 Corinthians, Romans, and Ephesians particularly.

B. OUTREACH MINISTRIES

The hospitality of a congregation, if it in any way mirrors the hospitality of Jesus, will include those beyond the congregation who are in special need. The Scriptures seem to say that if persons can help themselves, they should; but if they can't, then it is the work of the church to be a servant to their need. "For all must carry their own loads," writes the apostle Paul (Galatians 6:5). Yet just a few lines before he counsels that we should "[b]ear one another's burdens, and in this way... fulfill the law of Christ" (Galatians 6: 2). In order to apply Paul's guidelines, we must discern the weight of the load and the strength of the person. In Matthew 25, Jesus makes it clear that there are persons in every community who cannot help themselves. Some are deprived of the physical necessities of life, with no way to earn a living; some are strangers, or sick, or imprisoned.

Each year a particular church council spent a "day apart," to plan for ministries in the next year. One year the question was raised, "Who is hurting in Centerville?" Sally spoke up. "I am!" Sally's husband had recently abandoned her and their three children. She was alone and far from her family in the midst of separation and divorce. Her suburban neighborhood had no resources to meet her need. The congregation responded. Four months later they had a drop-in center on Thursday nights for persons in Sally's situation. A year later a part-time counselor was hired. Today that ministry is a very effective, highly respected counseling center, specializing in family issues. The hospitality of that congregation to persons in need has resulted in a significant number of people who have found healing. Some have moved from counseling into the community of the congregation.

In another congregation the question about who is hurting would have been answered, "Parents who must work and find day care they can trust." Today that congregation sponsors the best day care center, nursery schools, and kindergarten in the area.

Who is hurting in your community? Is the need of these persons being met by government or community agencies, or by other congregations? Many government services are being curtailed or dropped. What can your congregation do? Your ability to serve will, of course, depend on what you learn as you study the issue and face it in prayer. Survey the gifts in your congregation, including the space that is available. Consider also the space available elsewhere in the community. A congregation can make use of space in other places than the church building. In one community a city-owned building was leased for a dollar a year for a church-sponsored, city-wide youth ministry.

Is there a need for housing? Some congregations are participating in a "hospitality network." They and other congregations each take one night a week on a rotating basis. Shelter is provided in church facilities for homeless persons. A growing number of congregations are joining together to look for long-term solutions to the problem of homelessness. Some build houses through Habitat for Humanity. Some repair homes through the Appalachian Service Project[31] and other agencies. There is, of course, a serendipity in this kind of hospitality, namely the experience of hosting the holy in our midst. Jesus himself said, "'Truly I tell you, just as you did it to one of the least of these who are members of my family, you did it to me'" (Matthew 25:40).

The first Christians, like Abraham and Sarah, received blessings when they shared their faith by practicing hospitality. They "entertained angels without knowing it" (Hebrews 13:2). That same blessing is available to us and to our congregations as we

---

[31] The Appalachian Service Project is an affiliate organization of the General Board of Discipleship of The United Methodist Church. Especially designed to offer youth opportunities for service, the ASP s. ministry is renovating housing and providing new housing. They may be reached at 4523 Bristol Highway, Johnson City, TN 37601; 423-854-8800; www.asphome.org.

welcome others into the family of God and celebrate the gifts of ministry and service.

• • •

On the following page you are invited to name the intentional ministries in your congregation by which you welcome people, help them to belong, and equip persons to be conscious disciples of Jesus Christ.

"Do not neglect to show hospitality to strangers for thereby some have entertained angels unawares"
Hebrews 13:2.

WELCOMING

1. _____

2. _____

3. _____

4. _____

5. _____

BELONGING

1. _____

2. _____

3. _____

4. _____

5. _____

DISCIPLING

1. _____

2. _____

3. _____

4. _____

5. _____

SHARING FAITH THROUGH PERSONAL RELATIONSHIPS AND STORIES

"So faith comes from what is heard, and what is heard comes through the word of Christ"
(Romans 10:17).

If you have read the previous chapter you need not be reminded that relationships are vital in the whole process of welcoming, belonging, and discipling. These relationships are important to our primary task as we help persons relate to God and be initiated into the reign of God. The truth is, people do not come to Christ or the church on their own or become related to God or nurtured on their own. Neither are they sent out on their own.

In every study the central influences in Christian faith formation have been people. When groups have been asked, "Who influenced your faith journey most?" the responses invariably are the names of persons with whom participants have had close relationships. As Paul says, "faith comes from what is heard," (Romans 10:17), and what is heard comes through the relationship, word spoken, and life lived by other people in our network of associations. Within the context of the faith-sharing congregation, people are nurtured in faith so their individual and collective acts of hospitality will inspire others.

We have said that congregations tell the good news of Christ through the practice of hospitality. As we have seen, the core process of a faith-sharing congregation includes welcoming (reaching and receiving people), belonging (relating people to God and nurturing them in the faith), and discipling (growing in discipleship and being sent into the community to make it more loving and just). In every congregation people leave the pews and have countless contacts out in the world, but they hesitate to bring their own faith life into the open. Thus they lose their chance to participate in the ministry of invitation, and the evangelical flow is obstructed: the core process is blocked. There is a brokenness in the area of belonging or nurturing when people cannot identify their own faith story. This results in their not inviting others. Laity need to be equipped for faith sharing, so they can share faith and hospitality both in the congregation and in the world.

Therefore, important tasks for the faith-sharing congregation are to help people understand the importance of open sharing; to identify their own faith story; and to encourage and help others tell of the doubts, the disappointments, and the loving care they have known along life's pathway. This is how persons are trained in sharing faith.

As part of a Lay Witness Mission, participants are invited to spend a few moments reflecting on their faith journey. They are then asked to tell something of that story. Sometimes a person will claim to have no story to share. When invited to clarify, they often respond that they have not had a dramatic conversion like Paul on the Damascus road. Therefore, they feel they have no story.

In our passion to affirm both the transforming power of God's Spirit and the possibility for change that each person has in Jesus Christ, we may do a disservice to some people. That story of Paul's conversion has been told and retold. We remember it as the dramatic model of a powerful new life in Christ. Perhaps it is the sheer drama of Paul's story that has led some to conclude that this is the only model for conversion and changed life.

Studies indicate that by the year 2000, half of the adults in the United States will not have been nurtured in the church. These adults will not know the names of the four Gospels. They will not be familiar with biblical stories. They will not even know who Paul is. Some of these persons may be able to see their own experience relating to Paul's story. But first they need to hear it. And among the people who find their way into the Christian family, many, perhaps the majority, will have come to faith in other ways. Their lifestyles will not need to exhibit the dramatic change of Paul's. We see in the Scriptures a variety of ways persons came to faith in Jesus Christ. Paul's story is only one.

PAUL'S STORY

Everything about his story was dramatic. It is a story of coming to faith in which the inner, total reorientation to life is outwardly manifest and very dramatically experienced and evidenced within a short time.

As Saul of Tarsus, he was convinced that the people called Christian were wrong. He was present at, and probably participated in, the violence of stoning people to death. The Scripture says that "Saul was ravaging the church by entering house after house; dragging off both men and women, he committed them to prison" (Acts 8:3).

Sometimes when we read the Bible and it feels like a story from so long ago, we tend to miss the full impact of the account. In order to bring the reality of Paul's story closer, think for a moment about similar acts in our own time. Remember the holocaust and the men, women, and children who were sent to concentration camps, to work camps, often to their death. Similarly, it wasn't long ago in the United States that African Americans were dragged from their homes without trial and lynched by otherwise "respectable" citizens, some who even claimed the name of Christian. Likewise, during the Second World War, American-born and naturalized Japanese American citizens were taken to "relocation centers" and their property was confiscated.

All of these acts were committed in the last half century. The deeds were carried out by people who had made commitments to various social, religious, or patriotic causes, based on information they had heard and examined. These are the kinds of atrocities in which Saul was involved. He was educated, and he, too, had clearly examined the issues and had come to conclusions he felt were well founded.

On the Damascus road, Paul was called to re-examine his convictions. We can only imagine the kind of inner struggle that must have gone on during those intense days.

The convictions of Paul changed. The way in which he acted on those convictions changed. No longer was Paul involved in physical violence and persecution as he shared the gospel. What had not changed was the intensity of his beliefs. There are other persons throughout history who, like Paul, have experienced a dramatic change through the transforming power of the living Christ. Even today there are remarkable stories that show the Holy Spirit's power and presence in our midst.

TIMOTHY'S STORY

Paul's friend and associate, Timothy, was nurtured in faith within his family. Paul wrote to his younger friend:

> *Recalling your tears, I long to see you so that I may be filled*
> *with joy. I am reminded of your sincere faith, a faith that lived*
> *first in your grandmother Lois and your mother Eunice and*
> *now, I am sure, lives in you. For this reason, I remind you to*
> *rekindle the gift of God that is within you through the laying*
> *on of my hands; for God did not give us a spirit of cowardice,*
> *but rather a spirit of power and of love and of self-discipline*
> (2 Timothy 1:4-7).

One wonders what Timothy had been experiencing that Paul referred to his tears. Had Timothy said something to Paul through letter or messenger? Had others told Paul something about Timothy? Had he become discouraged as he tried to tell the world around him about Jesus and the people of the Way? Had Paul's own situation become one of discouragement and pain for Timothy?

Paul's letter was one of encouragement. He affirmed Timothy's "sincere faith." He reminded Timothy of the faith of his mother and grandmother. Lois and Eunice must have been known for their faithfulness, maybe even for their faithfulness in praying for their son and grandson, Timothy.

Timothy's own faith was undoubtedly nurtured by the ways he saw his mother and grandmother model a life of discipleship. In Timothy we have a Christian brought to commitment through nurture in his own immediate family. Timothy's story is a critical model today. It can help to enable people to comprehend more fully the importance of the family in nurturing and bringing one to the Christian faith.

PETER'S STORY

In the story of Peter, we see yet a third way that persons come to faith. Peter followed immediately when Jesus called him. Peter was among Jesus' inner circle. His story exemplifies the faith journey of one who believes that Jesus is the revelation of God. Unlike Paul, steady confidence and faith in Jesus were not easy for Peter.

In some of the biblical narrative, it is evident that Peter had not caught the essence of Jesus' message about the nature of the reign of God. Peter was among the disciples who, even in the time around the Last Supper, was asking "What's in it for me?" Luke's account says the disciples were arguing among themselves "as to which of them was to be regarded as the greatest" (Luke 22:24). Peter was probably there. Though the message of Jesus is one of a society in which God's grace and generosity is offered to all, Peter struggled with a desire for position and possession as a reward for his faithfulness.

Doubt was also part of Peter's journey. He was with the disciples in the boat that had been tossed about and battered by the winds. In the midst of the storm, Jesus appeared to them. In Matthew 14:25-33 we can read of one of many times Peter doubted. For a moment he found himself walking on the water at Jesus' invitation. Even as Peter's faith allowed him quickly to respond to Jesus, he doubted once again. He took his eyes off Jesus and began to sink.

Peter's story is not just one of doubt and struggle. His is a story of denial and turning away from Jesus. There was a turning away from Jesus in the Garden of Gethsemane. When Jesus needed so much to have his close friends pray with him, they slept. But a far more serious turning away was Peter's denial of Jesus when Jesus needed his support the most.

Fortunately, that was not the end of Peter's story. Once again Jesus met Peter by the lakeshore and once again spoke the words of invitation, "'Follow me'" (John 21:19). Peter went on to have as powerful and influential a ministry as Paul. The Scriptures say: "Yet more than ever believers were added to the Lord, great numbers of both men and women, so that they even carried out the sick into the streets, and laid them on cots and mats, in order that Peter's shadow might fall on some of them as he came by" (Acts 5:14-15). Peter was not ashamed of the gospel. He grew bold in his witness, in naming the name of Jesus. His confidence was not in himself but in the power of the Living Christ.

THEOLOGICAL PRINCIPLES

There are at least two theological principles in the Bible that form a foundation for focusing on the variety of ways people come to faith. The first is diversity. Diversity is as much a part of creation as we saw hospitality was in Chapter 2. So, we see in creation the diversity of humanity and of plant and animal life, which God called good.

We see diversity at the points of redemption in the New Testament. We saw this first in the three stories of ways persons come to faith. We see it second in the ways Jesus approached people. He did not have one question for all. Rather, he saw in people their individual needs and the points of brokenness in their lives. To the religious leader he said, "'You must be born from above'" (John 3:7). To the woman at the well, he said, "'Go call your husband'" (John 4:16). To the woman caught in adultery, he asked, "'Where are they (your accusers)? Has no one condemned you? Go your way and do not sin again'" (John 8:10-11). To the rich young ruler, he said, "'sell your possessions and give the money to the poor'" (Matthew 19:21). To Zacchaeus, he said, "'I must stay at your house today'" (Luke 12:5). Each person had a different need, and Jesus used a variety of questions and challenges. We see diversity in the ways he met individuals at their point of need and challenged them to radical transformation.

The second theological assumption is that Christian faith formation, though diverse, is always relational. Faith is relational because God created human beings in God's image and continues to relate to God's people.

Faith is relational in the story of Jesus. God could have deserted humanity and creation in their unfaithfulness. But in the New Testament we have the story of a God who cared so much that God came as Emmanuel, "God with us." Do we not need someone with us, both when life is filled with joy and celebration and when we know pain? That someone, God incarnate, was and is Jesus. God's great compassion and love for humanity is unfathomable: "God so loved the world that he gave his only Son, so that everyone who believes in him may not perish but may not perish but may have eternal life" (John 3:16). God so loved! God's story continues to be one of relationship with God's world.

SIGNIFICANCE OF RELATIONSHIPS

In each of the faith models discussed earlier, we can see the importance and significance of relationships. Timothy's faith was nurtured through significant relationships with his mother and grandmother as well as with Paul. Surely Paul had been influenced by the faith acted out by Christians—Stephen most of all— as they were being persecuted. In his state of blindness Paul's beginnings in his growth toward the Christian faith were brought to greater focus and understanding through a relationship with Ananias. Later, persons like Barnabas helped that new faith keep growing. It took courage to stand with Paul when others in the early church, with good reason, had difficulty believing the reality of his transformation. Could they forget the terror he had brought upon them?

Peter's story also is grounded in his relationships with Jesus and the Twelve Apostles. We see in the Gospel accounts the basic relationship of trust that was formed. Christian formation cannot be separated from significant relationships in life.

Remember the story (in Acts 3:1-10) in which Peter and John meet a man outside the temple at the Beautiful Gate? This was not the man's first time in that place. He had been carried there for years by people to beg from those who were entering the temple. The scene was no different on that day. Peter and John were just two of those who walked near the man. He asked for money. They stopped. They looked at him and directed him to look at them. He expected them to give him coins. But Peter and John had none to offer. While his financial need was real, Peter and

John offered words of healing in the name of Jesus and then reached out to assist the man to his feet. They reached out to him in hospitality. What a gift they received! The man was dancing and leaping and shouting with joy, praising the living God for his new life. The way we relate to people is an extension of our theology of hospitality. In and through that kind of relationship, God's Spirit can work within us and others with greater freedom and empowerment.

Formation in the Christian faith is relational not only because God is relational with us, but also because we come to faith through significant interpersonal relationships. Ours is a relational faith because we are not Christians in isolation. In the early church the homes of individual Christians became "house churches" where those of the faith could relate to one another. Christianity brought people to radical ways of being faithful. No longer was the center of religious life based on the sacrificial system of the temple. The new focus was on being a family in Christ. This was a major paradigm shift. Because of the missionary nature of the church, those who belonged to Christ needed to be together. Throughout history when the church has experienced persecution, Christians have needed to come together for support and encouragement. In that period known as Christendom, when it was assumed that the society was Christian and was living by "Christian values", attendance at worship had faltered. We are once again in a missionary time.

Christians prayed together, encouraged one another, and, after witnessing in the world, came back together. Paul and others felt responsible for these groups and found intentional ways to encourage and nurture Christian formation. To enter the reign of God is to relate to a community of faith whose purpose is to participate with God in moving toward God's vision of shalom and wholeness for all God's creation. Tertullian is said to have stated that "he cannot have God as father who does not have church as mother."

Within faith formation there is an integrity of redemption found in the action of God's Spirit. As in the story of Peter, in the story of Paul, too, it is very clear that he was empowered by the Holy Spirit—that transformation had taken place because of and in the name of Jesus Christ. It was not of his own doing, his own works.

GOD'S SPIRIT TRANSFORMS

We live in a time of individualism. Many see only the importance of the end goal and do not see the importance of integrity in the means and process for reaching that goal. Lest we assume that we can chart our own course, it is even more important to remember the role of the Holy Spirit in our spiritual journey.

Some churches ask that persons who come forward to receive

Holy Communion hold their hands out to receive the elements. When the church serves by intinction, the server places the bread in the hands of the ones who come. For many, the symbolism of this is rich; they are reminded that redemption is not of their own works. Our faith grows as we are willing to receive God's grace, God's guidance, God's Spirit.

One way we can assist people in this understanding is through the symbolism and images formed by our language. It is important that the language we use in the secular world to invite persons into a relationship with the living Christ express not what we do to persons but what the Holy Spirit calls forth in relationships.

Out of a passion that persons know a relationship with the living Christ, we have often spoken of "winning persons for Christ." This phrase came out of a deep conviction that the living Christ makes a difference in our lives today. As seen in the New Testament, Christ was understood to be the way to salvation and wholeness. That conviction still remains, but along the way the image of winning persons to Christ has sometimes been warped by a change in culture and cultural understanding.

Today, "winning" is understood as our personal achievement or good fortune. Winning is something we do. It is equated with a competition in which we are the conquerors, the victors over someone else. When we win we receive trophies and medals and ribbons to place on our walls and in our showcases. The passion and conviction has not lessened, but maybe we need to look at the language we use, particularly for those outside the church who do not understand our religious terms.

The Wesleyan theology of "prevenient grace" clearly reminds us that God's action comes first in the lives of people. God's Spirit is already at work in people's lives before they make a commitment to Christ, before they recognize the importance of a relationship with Christ. In prevenient grace the Holy Spirit is active in the life of a person even before others share the gospel or their own faith story or even invite them to meet Jesus. The work of the Holy Spirit in one's life is what stirs the yearning for God, that brings forth the awareness that entering the reign of God can fill the emptiness of life and bring salvation and wholeness.

INVITING THROUGH OUR RELATIONSHIPS

We understand without question that most people who come to faith and who continue in their relationship with the church were invited and encouraged by another person or persons. An important part of the goal should be not only that persons come, but also they remain in relationship.

In John 11:1-44 there is the story of Lazarus, brother of Mary and Martha. He was seriously ill and his sisters sent for Jesus. Lazarus died and had been in the tomb before Jesus arrived. As Jesus stood with Mary and Martha and others at the tomb, he asked them to take the stone from the entry to the tomb. But, with that done, it was Jesus, not the others, who called forth Lazarus from the tomb. It is Jesus who calls us forth from death to life. Lazarus came out, still bound with cloth from burial. In that moment Jesus asked those nearby to unwrap Lazarus and free him (John 11:38-44). While the initiative is God's, we are called to be in relationship with others, so that in partnership with God we might invite and nurture them in faith development.

One of the ways many churches encourage people to invite others is through FRANgelism or the Friends, Relatives, Acquaintances, Neighbors plan. Persons in the congregation are invited to write down those within their network who are not part of any church. They list a friend, a relative, an associate, and a neighbor. This process can be done during a worship service as a response to the word.

People are asked to pray for those they have listed, to make contact with them in conversation or letter, to share faith with them in intentional ways, and to invite them to participate in worship and the life of the church. Often the F-R-A-N plan is used during a particular season of the year: Advent, Lent, from Easter to Pentecost. The F-R-A-N plan is a tool to remind us of the importance of all persons sharing faith and inviting others within their everyday environment. (See the next page for a diagram of the FRAN plan.)[32] A Personal FRAN plan brochures are available from Discipleship Resources, 800-972-0433.

---

[32] Donald W. Haynes, *Vision 2000: The Western North Carolina Story* (Nashville, Tennessee: The Section on Evangelism General Board of Discipleship, 1993), p. 41. FRAN Plan copyrighted by Donald W. Haynes, 1992.

FRAN
A Ministry for Reaching the Unchurched

Who is unchurched? Anyone who cannot recall the incumbent pastor's name! Or, anyone who has not been to his or her church in six months!

FRIEND	**RELATIVE**
Name	Name
Address	Address
Phone	Phone

Your Name

ACQUAINTANCE	**NEIGHBOR**
Name	Name
Address	Address
Phone	Phone

COVENANT:
- ❏ I shall pray for these persons daily.
- ❏ I shall invite them to church and offer to bring them.

RECOVERING PERSONAL FAITH STORIES

One of the vital ways congregations share faith is in the equipping of people to verbalize their faith stories. In our work, which has taken us to many congregations, we sometimes ask the question, "What are the barriers to your sharing faith?" People's answers have fallen into three categories. One: there are great misconceptions and misunderstandings about what it means to evangelize. People hold a negative stereotype of evangelism and witnessing and are unable to move beyond that. They have good reasons for not wanting to fall into the negative stereotypes of these actions. Two: this category consists of people's sense of need for education, training, and experience before evangelizing. The third category is characterized by expressions such as, "I am afraid of what others might think of me"; "To me it isn't really important that people know about Christ, especially if they are already good and decent people"; and "I don't have any opportunities to share my faith."

While it is important for the church to address all of these issues, the first task is to help people identify their story. There are several ways through which churches can help persons identify their own faith story and feel more comfortable talking about it. Some churches include an opportunity to witness during the worship service every Sunday or at least once a month. Individuals are given a specific amount of time and asked to talk about a current experience and how faith made a difference.

Other churches have a time at the start of church council and other official meetings when people are invited to talk about where they have seen God at work in their own lives and in the world in the last week. They are asked to mention joys and concerns, and to spend a few moments in prayer. Sometimes the pastor asks the members of the group to tell one other person when and how they had seen God at work. That not only helps persons to practice talking about their faith; it helps them to develop the skills necessary for listening. The experience of hearing one another's story and praying together form the foundation for keeping a spiritual dimension to the discussion and decisions to come.

We need communities of faith that are seen as safe places for people to share their problems or doubts without fear of being judged. Where are the places we encourage people to identify and talk about their own faith stories? In many Sunday school classes and small groups, people are encouraged to study the biblical stories, to review the heritage or to talk about God but seemingly always outside their own experience of the living Christ and their own life of discipleship. Christians need not only to be able to talk about faith, about faith stories, but also to witness to the power of the living Christ in their own journeys.

A Model for Equipping Laity

The following is a possible model that can be used in small groups to help people identify and tell their own faith journey. You can help people discover and deepen their faith story by focusing on these questions.

The first question to ask is "Who?" Who is the person who had most to do with your being a Christian? Many people respond to this question by remembering their father or mother, an aunt or an uncle. Who was it for you? Was it one of those mentioned? Was it another member of your family? Was it a spouse, a friend, a business associate? Point out what should have been obvious, but probably is not: very rarely is anyone led to faith by a stranger. Some additional questions that could be used in amplifying the "who question": How did this person help you come to the Christian faith? What were the characteristics of this person that drew you into relationship with him or her?

The second question begins with "When." When, along the way in your life, have you experienced moments in which your relationship with the living Christ truly made a difference? Why was this particular moment so significant in your faith? In the Saturday night small groups of Lay Witness Missions, people are asked to begin to identify their personal faith story by answering the above questions and using a "spiritual autobiography chart."[33]

MY SPIRITUAL AUTOBIOGRAPHY

In the form of a chart, diagram, or other graphic display, illustrate your spiritual journey from your earliest memory to the present. Indicate with an "X" the points where God was most real to you. At what points have you been most faithful?

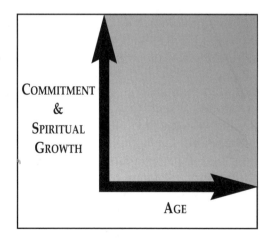

COMMITMENT & SPIRITUAL GROWTH

AGE

---

[33] "My Spiritual Autobiography", *The Lay Witness Mission Handbook* (Nashville, Tennessee: Discipleship Resources, 1993), p. 32. Used with permission from Discipleship Resources, Nashville, TN.

A third question to use in identifying one's faith story will begin with"What?" What is your current experience as a faith sharer? What are the ways in which you are growing in faith? What are the ways in which your relationship to the living Christ makes different your daily living, relationships, lifestyle, and decisions? What are the ways in which you hear God in prayer, in the Bible, and in everyday?

Helping people share their faith story is more than helping them write an autobiography. We invite them to tell their story, pointing to the living Christ as active in the drama of their life. Sharing our faith is more than an interesting exercise. It is a way of rehearsing the story we have to tell so the center of our journey, our relationship with Jesus Christ, remains the center. Sharing our faith journey and the ways we feel God's nudging and prodding in our lives helps us clarify the word we are hearing. Perhaps it is not God's word. Speaking our story out loud is a way of participating in mutual accountability with others in the faith community and even with the stranger.

RESOURCES FOR HELPING PEOPLE SHARE FAITH

A valuable resource for training persons in faith sharing is called, quite appropriately, the *Faith-Sharing Video Kit*.[34] It is a six-session training using a book and a video that contain both input from lecturers and vignettes of persons in real-life situations. It is often used in small groups for new members as well as for persons in the congregation who are ready to learn to share their faith more effectively in their daily living. This has also been used as a follow-up to the DISCIPLE Bible Study.[35] Some congregations have adapted the Faith-Sharing study to use in a retreat or weekend seminar.

One pastor has small groups that are studying the Scriptures. To help persons grow in their faith-sharing skills, he invites them to read and re-read the specific passage for each day. Their assignment during the week is to see how this relates to their faith and to faith sharing. They report their insights at the beginning of the next session.

Some pastors have used *A Ministry of Caring*[36] as a resource for training persons in the skills of faith sharing. The resource includes help in connecting one's story with the biblical story.

Many congregations have used the Lay Witness Mission as a way to help persons identify their own faith story as visiting laity

---

[34] *Faith-Sharing Video Kit* (DR207) is available from Discipleship Resources, 1-800-972-0433.

[35] *DISCIPLE Bible Study* is an in-depth Bible study designed to develop leadership and strengthen faith in youth and adults who participate. For more information call 1-800-672-1789 or write to *DISCIPLE Bible Study*, P. O. Box 801, Nashville, TN 37202-0801.

[36] *A Ministry of Caring* includes a Leader s Guide (DR290) and a Participant s Workbook (DR289). These are available from Discipleship Resources,1-800-972-0433 or www.discipleshipresources.org.

tell their stories.[37] Other evangelism strategies for the local church include the Faith-Sharing Initiative, *Witness,* and the Key Event Celebration. They offer assistance in helping laity to identify their own faith story, understand how that story intersects with God's story, and find new encouragement in reaching out to others.[38]

MOTIVATION FOR FAITH SHARING AND HOSPITALITY

If asked why they share their faith, most Christians would quote the great commission, "Go therefore and make disciples of all nations, baptizing them in the name of the Father and of the Son and of the Holy Spirit, and teaching them to obey everything that I have commanded you" (Matthew 28:19-20). As Christians, we cannot ignore our calling and commission. However, there is a deeper and prior motivation for sharing the good news of Jesus Christ.

The same prior issue as to why persons need to share faith can be found in the Old Testament as well. In Exodus, God gave to Moses and then to the people religious and social laws for living together (Exodus 20:1-17). We often miss the introduction to the Ten Commandments and, therefore, miss the critical issue of motivation.

The passage begins with God's words: "'I am the Lord your God, who brought you out of the land of Egypt, out of the house of slavery'" (Exodus 20:2). God asked the people to obey the law, because God was their God, the Holy One who brought them out of bondage. It had been a long, hard life and journey. It was not over yet, but God reminded them of the great gift they had been given. Therefore, in a response of thanksgiving and gratitude they were asked to follow the religious and social rules for living in God's world. The people were asked to respond not just because the message was from God; they were invited to live a life of response to the love and guidance and freedom they had been given by God.

Jesus made this clear as well. John's gospel includes a conversation between Jesus and Peter:

> *Jesus said to Simon Peter, "Simon son of John, do you love me more than these?" He said to him, "Yes, Lord; you know that I love you." Jesus said to him, "Feed my lambs." A second time he said to him, "Simon son of John, do you love me?" He said to him, "Yes, Lord; you know that I love you." Jesus said to him, "Tend my sheep." He said to him the third time, "Simon son of John, do you love me?" Peter felt hurt because he said to*

---

[37] For more information, go to the Evangelism page on the General Board of Discipleship web site (www.gbod.org/evangelism) or write to Lay Witness Mission, General Board of Discipleship, The United Methodist Church, P.O. Box 340003, Nashville, TN 37203-0003.

[38] For more information, go to the Evangelism page on the General Board of Discipleship web site (see note 37) or write to the program (Faith-Sharing Initiative, *Witness,* Key Event) at the above address.

*him the third time, "Do you love me?" And he said to him,
"Lord, you know everything; you know that I love you." Jesus
said to him, "Feed my sheep"*
(John 21:15-17).

The question Jesus asked of Peter he asks of us: "'Do you love
me?'" "'Do you love me?'" It is out of our love for Jesus that we
are asked to serve, to share the good news. Our response of
thanksgiving and love for what God has already done for us in
Jesus Christ is the motivation for evangelizing the gospel. The
love about which Jesus questioned Peter was not a limp, wimpy
kind of love. At the end of that passage Jesus told Peter of the
persecutions for the faith and the death Peter would die. When
Jesus asked Peter, "'Do you love me?'" he was asking about a
deep, costly love.

The question of motivation is a critical one. The Christian faith
is relational. Think of one of the most significant relationships in
your life. Think of the ways you and that person care for one
another and relate to one another. Does it not make a difference
in that relationship and in the way the caring takes place if you
do it out of love and thanksgiving rather than out of a sense of
obligation? So it is in our Christian journey.

During the Last Supper (John 13:1-20) Jesus set an example of
extraordinary and extravagant love. He and his Disciples had all
arrived at the place for their meal. Jesus was Teacher, yet not one
of the Disciples had completed the hospitable and common act of
washing feet. Jesus got up to care for this act of kindness and
welcome. He washed the feet of one who was to deliver him to
death and one who was to openly deny him in order to protect
himself. He washed the feet of those who had argued about the
place next to Him in the kingdom, not understanding the kind of
reign Jesus had been talking about.

That act of foot washing was a radical kind of love. Jesus
invited the Disciples to follow that humbling, self-giving love in
response to what he had already done for them. After that act,
Jesus spoke to the group. He said, "'So if I, your Lord and
Teacher, have washed your feet, you also ought to wash one
another's feet. For I have set you an example, that you also
should do as I have done to you'" (John 13:14-15).

Again in John, Jesus spoke to the Disciples: "'If you love me,
you will keep my commandments'" (John 14:15). The clear message of the biblical account, in both the Old Testament and the
New Testament, is that God has acted in our behalf. God has
given amazing grace and love in Jesus Christ. God continues to
invite us to receive grace and salvation and wholeness. In our
response of thanksgiving and gratitude, because we love the God

who was shown to us in Jesus, we, too, love and participate with God in inviting others to see and enter the reign of God.

This is the foundation of the core process of faith-sharing congregations as we reach out and receive persons. As we have seen, however, in the ministry of belonging and discipling, the leader in the process has responsibility for helping people to identify their own faith story, in some cases to recall it to memory, and for equipping them to share faith and invite others. Whether this ministry of hospitality is done within the context of the faith-sharing congregation gathered or in the community as the faithful are scattered, the equipping of the saints for sharing faith is crucial to the evangelical flow.

Sharing Faith in the Domestic Church

*"....both the 'communal church' and the 'domestic church' need
to recapture a vision of the Christian family as a sacred community."*
Marjorie J. Thompson, Family: The Forming Center[39]

The faith-sharing congregation helps families learn how to be centers of faith formation. In the vision of the leadership it is important to remember nurturing and sending are parts of the primary task, identified on page vi and page 12. The congregation as evangelist is critical as it models church for the family and household. This is important: the faith community is not only existent when the people are gathered. We have often referred to the church gathered, then to the church scattered as they go into the world, sent as disciples to make the world a more loving and just place. However, it is also important to see faith *community* as existent not only in the gathering of the people in the building called the church but also in the families and households of the faithful. The church, the community of faith, is both communal and domestic.

The "communal church," the gathering of the faith community, is the place where we struggle with being—and understanding what it means to be—the community of Christ. It is people together, in the name of Christ, sometimes experiencing the reality of hospitality and sometimes offering that experience to others.

---

[39] Marjorie J. Thompson, *Family: The Forming Center* (Nashville, Tennessee: Upper Room, 1989), p. 26.

The communal church includes those who sometimes are centered enough in the living Christ to welcome one another in all their differences and diversities. At other times we painfully recognize the negative and hurtful results of our humanness as we try to live together in Christ. The communal church, in its ideal form, shows biblical hospitality and models sacred community.

The communal church serves as resource to its constituent families and households. Even in its weakness and struggle, the communal church offers an invitation to its families to catch glimpses of the vision of what it means to be a sacred community in which the reign of God is seen. The family or household that can capture the vision through the communal church may be enabled to be a sacred community, a "domestic church," in its own existence, as it, too, struggles to offer hospitality and welcome to the stranger. For the domestic church as well as for the communal church, the stranger may already be in its midst. Not on Sunday alone, but in the constancy of everyday life, the family and household much more profoundly model the experience by which we understand our own centeredness in Christ. The family and household are places where we are formed and re-formed in the faith. Our everyday experiences shape us. If we take seriously the possibility of family being "domestic church," family will be given a greater valuation by the communal church as a place to assist people in growing in understanding and experience of hospitality.

Family, in this context, is defined as however people constitute themselves in basic living and support units. This includes the nuclear family as well as the other configurations in our culture today.

FAITH AND FAMILY IN THE OLD TESTAMENT

From the beginning, faith was understood as corporate in the Judeo-Christian tradition. Faith was shared and worship took place in the family and larger community. The early Scriptures are the stories of God speaking to individuals with messages for the whole nation. The faith was always a faith for the family, for the community, for the people of God, and for the life of the nation. There has always been a healthy tension between the larger community and the family as the center for faith formation. But our roots are in a heritage where family has primacy as the place where faith stories are told and faith is formed.

In the early history of the faith, the patriarch shared the blessing with the family, particularly with the sons. Once the blessing—the offering of the future—was given to a child, it could not be taken back. So, the blessing of the faith, of the land, of the family, and of the future was shared through the family. Later, when Israel went into exile, the home remained the primary place for sharing the nation's story. The story of the Exodus, in particular, was central to the family ritual known as Seder. Children learned the history of God's actions through stories told and retold within their families. The Scriptures remind us of the importance of the rituals and symbols that invite the questions of children. In Joshua is the story of the people crossing the Jordan. God told Joshua to have representatives of the twelve tribes pick up a stone as they crossed through the Jordan. It was to be a sign. Joshua selected the twelve and gave them instructions. When the stones were piled on the other side, the people began to ask "Why?" Joshua replied, "'When your children ask their parents in time to come, "What do these stones mean?" then you shall let your children know, "Israel crossed over the Jordan here on dry ground." For the Lord your God dried up the waters of the Jordan for you until you crossed over'" (Joshua 4:21-22). The visibility of the symbols and signs of faith was important. When children asked about them, there was an opportunity to tell what God had done for them and for their ancestors before them.

Edward Hays says:

> *The first altar around which primitive people worshipped was the hearth, whose open-fire burned in the center of the home. The next altar-shrine was the family table where meals were celebrated and great events in the personal history of the family were remembered. The priests and the priestesses of these first rituals were the fathers and mothers of families.*[40]

The family and home, whether a "permanent" residence or in the tents of the pilgrim people, was the place of primary spiritual formation for people beginning in childhood.

FAITH AND FAMILY IN THE NEW TESTAMENT

Jesus broadened the understanding of family expressed by some in the crowds around him. In Matthew we find the story of Jesus' mother and brothers standing on the edges of the crowd while he was speaking. Someone told Jesus his family was there, probably thinking, since they were his family, he would more quickly disengage himself from the crowds. His response was, "'Who is my mother, and who are my brothers?' And, pointing to his disciples, he said, 'Here are my mother and my brothers! For whoever does the will of my Father in heaven is my brother and sister and mother'" (Matthew 12:48-50).

Our first reaction may be one of amazement that Jesus would reject and turn away from his "family." *Perhaps our amazement should be that Jesus expanded even our understanding of family.* We will

---

[40] Edward Hays, *Prayers for the Domestic Church: A Handbook for Worship in the Home* (Leavenworth, Kansas: Forest of Peace Publishing Inc., 251 Muncie Road., Leavenworth, KS 66048, 1979), p. 17.

look more closely at the importance of this as we explore the family in today's world later in the chapter.

There is great significance in the fact that the first meeting places were at the same "altar-shrines" where families ate and lived together. Likewise, in the New Testament, the family is critical to the sharing of faith. In the first centuries, house churches were started where families came together to pray, to study, to encourage one another, and to remember the stories of faith. In Ephesians there is an emphasis on the importance of life together in families and the relation of families to expressions of faith.

When we look at the New Testament church and the relationship between family and faith formation, we also remember Paul's word to the church in Corinth. In 1 Corinthians 7:25-40, Paul engages in a discourse about the benefits of celibacy. Of course, Paul was convinced he was living in the last days before the coming again of the Lord. There was an urgency about the ministry and about evangelizing the good news of Jesus Christ.

In this light, Paul's emphasis on celibacy was not for the sake of celibacy, nor was it a denial of the goodness of sexuality. Rather, the purpose was to achieve a more clear and more single-minded focus on God and on the purposes of God. Singleness was not a lifestyle for everyone, but it was a valid and valued lifestyle in the urgency of the times and for the gospel. Perhaps for some, then as now, the church became their primary family, the place where they found hospitality, welcome, and a sense of being at home with God.

THE FAMILY AND FAITH TODAY
Storytelling and Ritual

For the family then and now, the theological issue is not whether or not the family is engaged in faith formation. *The question is: What kind of formation is taking place?*

If faith formation is not attended to—if it is not a natural and normative part of life in the home—there is a strong likelihood there will be a dichotomy in the Christian faith journey between what happens in church and what happens in everyday life. The center of faith is not a set of beliefs or doctrines. The forming center of our life is that orientation out of which our lives are lived. The continuing formation of our lives in Jesus Christ enables our actions to express the invitation of God in Christ to be "at home" in Christ and to show hospitality.

What is the image of Christian discipleship that is operative in your family and in your home? Is there a difference between what is said and proclaimed and what is acted out? What does discipleship and ministry have to do with your work or vocation? How does your concept of discipleship affect the use of your money and how are these discussed as part of the family life?

The critical questions related to lifestyle and decision making become intensely personal questions for leaders who model discipleship. These are critical issues to be raised in offering resources to families and households for faith formation.

The theological issue in the relationship between family, home, and faith formation is how do we, in fact, live out the faith in our daily living? What are the rituals that are part of our family or life in our home that point to God and to faithfulness in our daily living? How do we model and express the hospitality of God? How is our home a welcoming place?

In Judaism there are traditional celebrations, festivals, and rituals that are a critical part of spiritual formation. There is a kind of "table spirituality." Rituals and prayers are used around the family table in which every member of the family has a significant role. During the Passover meal children have questions they ask. It is a way of rehearsing the story so the children learn about the actions of God in their history.

Rituals and symbols have the power to recall sacred moments and bring them into ordinary time with extraordinary meaning and grace. Rituals help us remember and bring forward into current time the sacred and holy moments that have shaped and transformed our lives. In ritual and symbol *kairos* and *chronos* merge. The quality and essence of the transcendent and mystery in God's acts—*kairos* moments—are experienced in real, quantitative time of now, *chronos*.

The Eastern Orthodox Church takes the role of the home in faith formation very seriously. There is a clear understanding that the home is the domestic church and the church gathered is the communal church. Thus, there is no dichotomy between the lived-out faith and the faith of the gathered. As the family gathers in its space, it is a portion of the body of Christ, and therefore it is church. In that tradition the house is blessed as a sign and symbol that the space is sacred and the church is present.[41]

What difference would it make for you if you participate in a house blessing as a way of understanding your home as sacred place, an ordinary space made holy? The house blessing is one of the rituals and symbols that has the potential to daily invite us back to our calling and to a remembrance of who we are as Christians.

Throughout the Judeo-Christian tradition, the home, the domestic church, has shared in the responsibility of being the storytellers of the faith. Today children often sit with grandparents or aunts and uncles or parents to hear stories. Adult children often ask their parents to rehearse the stories of the family that have helped to form them. One of the most meaningful and healing experiences that takes place immediately following the death

---

[41] Thompson, p. 124.

of a loved one is the telling of the stories of who that person has been and what significance he or she has had in the lives of others. Most cultures provide in the "good bye" ceremonies some variation of this practice in a scheduled visitation, in the wake, or in other similar rites.

The telling of stories forms and informs the teller as well as the ones who hear. The domestic church is the place for rehearsing the stories of the faith that help in the formation of who we are and who we shall yet become. There are also those stories that call us into the future promise. In this way visions of hope are shared and truths that shape our lifestyle and being are passed on to others.

What are the stories you rehearse and tell? Are they the stories of the faith or are they stories without connections to God's story?

Faith Formation

The place of the domestic church, the home, in faith formation today remains critical. The Search Institute, a research group in Minnesota primarily focused on religious data, did studies of adults and youth and the integration between their vertical relationship with God and their involvement in service to others. Data from those studies indicate that, for youth, while ongoing involvement in the Christian education ministries is important, the most critical factor related to a high degree of integrated faith is the family. The summary of that study reported:

> *The particular family experiences most tied to greater faith maturity are the frequency with which an adolescent talked with mother and father about faith, the frequency of family devotions, and the frequency with which parents and children together were involved in efforts, formal or informal, to help other people. Each of these family experiences is more powerful than the frequency with which an adolescent sees his or her parents engage in religious behavior like church attendance.*[42]

The second most important factor in the development of integrated faith is the ongoing involvement in Christian education ministries. Studies related to the incorporation of members into the life of the church also indicate the vital importance of involvement in a small group. A Sunday school class could be such a group, for adults as well as for youth and children.

The value of Christian education ministries is not in question. However, we recognize that with the growth of the Sunday school movement came an unforeseen and tragic consequence:

---

[42] Peter L. Benson and Carolyn H. Eklin, *Effective Christian Education: A national study of Protestant congregations - A summary report on faith, loyalty, and congregational life* (Minneapolis: Search Institute, 1990), p. 38.

As the movement progressed, the ministry of Christian education was seen less and less as an enhancement to faith formation in the home. Rather, many came to see Sunday school and Christian education as a replacement for what had formerly, in the Judeo-Christian tradition, taken place in the home. Christian education can be formational as well as informational. Even more important, however, is participation in the everyday nature of our faith through relationships that guide the members of the family. One dimension of that living is the welcome and hospitality offered in the home, both to those who live there and to those who are "strangers." Maturing faith formation occurs in the experience of finding a home in God and a place of hospitality.

Because the family is the center for faith formation, once again we are called to answer the question, "What kind of formation is taking place in your home and what kind of formation is it that you desire as persons growing in the image of Christ?"

William Willimon tells about a conversation he had with a rabbi who lived across the parking lot from him in Greenville, South Carolina. Willimon said his friend was part of a group with strong communal identity that was passed on to the children through families. When the children asked why they could not do the things their peers were doing, the reply was "That's fine for everyone else, but it's not fine for you. You are special. You are different. You are a Jew. We have different values, a different story."[43]

Should Christian faith formation in families be any less? We too are called to be different. We have a different story. We have a story of a God who lives today and who continues to act in history and calls us to faithful living. We have a story of One who offers hospitality and generosity to all. Within the family there are relationships, conversations, rituals, and symbols that enable us to grow toward being able to say with Paul, "it is no longer I who live, but it is Christ who lives in me" (Galatians 2:20).

As in the early stories of our Judeo-Christian faith, families are still the primary place where blessings are given that enable us to be integrated and whole persons. In the family we learn, through relationships, what love and commitment mean. We learn what it means to share hospitality, to offer the best we have to the stranger and to share God's love. By observing the congruity between the words and deeds of family members (or lack thereof), we learn what integrity means. By watching how decisions are based on values, we learn how the Story of God affects the lifestyle we live.

Families Today

When we talk about the family or domestic church, we realize that there is more than one image of that configuration. Some persons try to hold on to an Ozzie-and-Harriet image of a nuclear family of the 1950s: two parents, two children, and a dog who are always agreeable toward one another, who never argue, and for whom life's situations almost always have a happy ending with very few struggles of substance. The 2000 census records and other studies show more diversity than unanimity in family configurations.

In a family consultation held in Nashville, Tennessee, Dr. Brenda Dew, a professor at Vanderbilt University, gave the following statistics.

- The number of children under the age of eighteen who live in the homes of grandparents increased fifty percent over the two decades following the consultation. Many grandparents on fixed incomes now have an added expense of raising their own grandchildren.
- The norm is becoming a blended family, including children from the previous marriages of both spouses, or children from a previous relationship and the current marriage.
- Fifty-one percent of black households are headed by single parents.[44]

There are, of course, many families that mirror the traditional family lifestyle of two parents in their first marriage, living together with children in the same household. In many congregations the number of such families represents less than one half the total. Increasingly, in our congregations we see evidence of the following:

- Adult children living "back home." A phenomenon of the late 80s and the 1990s (and continuing) is the number of adult sons or daughters, some with and some without children, who go back to their parental home to live. In *Modern Maturity* two major articles included "When Kids Don't Leave" and a feature about a 70 year old woman raising three teenagers after the death of her brother.[45]
- Single parent households. A culture shift involves an increasing number of people who consider themselves to be settled and single. There are also people who are single but who do not see themselves as remaining single. Those who are divorced and those who are widowed would be included among singles.

---

[44] Brenda Dew, lecture at Family Ministries Consultation, September 9, 1994.
[45] "When Kids Don t Leave" and "Liz s Excellent Adventure," *Modern Maturity* Vol 35, (November-December, 1994).

- Couples who choose not to have children.
- Couples who live together and are not married. Some of these couples also have children.
- Couples who live apart. This living arrangement is often caused by their jobs.
- Older couples who live together. Often two older persons who would have chosen to marry discover that social security regulations, taxes, or inheritance laws would decrease their combined income if they married.
- Group living arrangements in large homes for older adults. This arrangement shows signs of becoming common as persons find in them mutual caring, companionship, and decreased living expenses.
- People in the workforce who share living space. This arrangement is often chosen when individuals do not have incomes adequate enough to live on their own. Sharing accommodations offers a way for such persons to live within their means and have a measure of companionship.
- People of the same sex who live and care for children together. The children in these families may be from previous marriages or may be adopted.

These are some of the realities of family and household configurations in today's world. Many of these lifestyles have for some time existed alongside the traditional family. Perhaps we have resisted acknowledging that many families and households were not, in fact, configured as we had always imagined them to be. Our culture is waking up to a reality that has been ignored. To be a "family church" today, as many congregations claim to be, is to take into consideration the variety of ways people form families and households. To continue to speak of family churches and design ministries as if everyone is in an Ozzie-and-Harriet family, will exclude ministry with many children, youth, and adults.

THE CHURCH AND THE FAMILY TODAY

Since the publication of Alex Haley's book *Roots* an African saying has become popular: "It takes a whole village to raise a child." In congregations that practice infant baptism, the congregation is expected to provide continuing support for the child. In United Methodist liturgy, for example, the congregation is invited to respond:

With God's help we will proclaim the good news
and live according to the example of Christ.

*We will surround **these persons***
with a community of love and forgiveness,
*that **they** may grow in **their** service to others.*

*We will pray for **them.***
*that **they** may be true disciples*
who walk in the way that leads to life.[46]

For each baby or child who is baptized while still too young to answer for himself or herself, the community of faith makes a covenant with the family and with God to help raise the child. To take this seriously is to live within the Judeo-Christian tradition of faith community and within the expanded vision of family that Jesus shared. While the family—the domestic church—is primary, the family of families—the communal church— shares the role of nurture and carries the responsibility of providing resources for the domestic church.

What would the picture look like if your church took this vow and responsibility seriously? What are ways your church can offer resources to the family?

OFFERING RESOURCES TO THE FAMILY

Sponsor/Friend

One example of a congregation taking their vow seriously is to have a "friend" from church visit a family before a child's birth. This friend offers support and resources to assist the family in providing a spiritually nurturing environment. Resources might include ideas, rituals, and actions that families may use to share God's love and nurture with the child, even as it is being formed in the womb. Such a friend would be important for all births, but particularly for the first child. This friend could be a sponsor or a representative of the congregation at the child's baptism.

Sponsors could also be assigned to those families who are planning to adopt or who are serving as foster parents.

Perhaps when family-selected godparents are from another congregation, or another area, the church could also provide sponsors from its membership. The sponsors could celebrate with the family, help to welcome a baby, and connect the family to the ministries the church provides to show care and nurture. One of the authors of this book remembers being asked to be a sponsor for the baby of friends who were in another denomination. That church was very clear that sponsors had more than perfunctory roles. Sponsors made covenant with the family, the church, and God to share in very specific responsibilities in the raising and nurturing of the child in the Christian faith.

When a family chooses sponsors for a child, what covenant do you ask them to enter into in the raising of the child? Who is the representative from the congregation who sees that the

---

[46] "The Baptismal Covenant II" in *The United Methodist Hymnal* (Nashville, Tennessee: The United Methodist Publishing House, 1989), p. 38. Copyright © 1976, 1980, 1985, 1989 The United Methodist Publishing House.

congregation fulfills the covenant made during the service of baptism?

To be a sponsor for a child at baptism, a congregational representative, is to take a role more important today than ever before. Extended families living in close proximity to one another are no longer the norm. These new roles enable adults to be substitute aunts, uncles, and grandparents. Children can learn to love and appreciate their roles as substitute nieces, nephews, and grand-children. In these ways the church can be the family of families which raises the child. The larger community, of course, does not replace the individual family in faith formation. Rather, the faith-sharing congregation extends a welcome and a home "village." The larger family, the church, can model hospitality in the home for the domestic church, the family.

Sign-acts in Baptism

One church presents a large candle to the family of each person being baptized. The individual's name and the date of the baptism are at the base of the candle. During the baptism the candle is lighted. The family is encouraged to celebrate the anniversary of the baptism by lighting the candle and telling the story. In another church a large shell is given to the family or person being baptized. The sanctuary walls of another church display banners to honor and celebrate the people received in baptism. An acquaintance of the authors took his child to the altar rail of the church each year to retell the story of the child's baptism and what that meant.

Baptism is the time when the communal family, the congregation, makes a covenant to help raise the infant or child in the faith. Many churches treat baptism as an add-on or an afterthought to the "main" worship. What if we would have a Service of Baptism as we have a Service of Holy Communion or the Eucharist, one in which the focus on baptism filled the whole service?

Some pastors use other ways to symbolize the importance of the covenant entered into by the people. An increasing number of pastors introduce the child to the congregation, often carrying or walking the child down the aisle into the congregation to symbolize the congregation's covenant. In some cases, that role is carried out by a lay person.

Ministries of Mentoring

Many churches use a mentoring ministry with youth, particularly during confirmation. Others use the mentoring ministry with youth throughout high school. Still other churches are beginning the mentoring ministry with children.

The Search Institute documents the importance of youth being able to talk and discuss faith and life concerns with their parents. That data also indicates that there are situations when youth are unable to have in-depth conversations with their parents. Such youth have a critical need for relationships with a caring adult, sometimes more than one, within the congregation.

A mentoring program is not a teaching, information-giving relationship; it is a mutual companionship in which each talks about his or her important questions and faith story. It is a ministry of listening as well as of sharing: "Mentoring relationships provide a place where it is more than OK to talk about personal questions of faith and life: It is positively encouraged."[47]

In a recent consultation on the family, two of the leaders stated that the ministry of listening is critical to spiritual formation and faith formation. In addition, they suggested that the lack of being listened to may be one of the major contributors to violence in our society today.

Several years ago a news reporter did a television interview with several persons who had been drug abusers and pushers. One person told the story of his transformation. A church in his city had begun a ministry of listening to the people on the street. The young man said he had grown to expect that people from religious and community organizations would tell him how bad he was and how awful his lifestyle was. But this was the first time anyone had come just to listen.

Even within the church, studies indicate that many youth feel they have no one with whom to talk when they need help or feel sad or depressed. Search Institute data states that 40 percent of youth say they rarely or never talk with their mother and 56 percent indicate they rarely or never talk with their father or relatives about their faith or about God.[48]

The communal church, if serious about helping youth to share faith and to grow in faith, will need to intentionally plan for ways to become family to its families. How can the communal church be in ministry with youth through adults who are significant others to them? How can the gathered church model hospitality to families in such a way families can be to others what they have experienced themselves, thus enabling them truly to be a domestic church?

MINISTRIES OF HOSPITALITY WITH CHILDREN

In an earlier chapter we focused on hospitality and on the valuing of all persons. Here we want to focus on how the communal

---

[47] Charles Kishpaugh and Barbara Bruce, *Friends in Faith: Mentoring Youth in the Church* (Nashville, Tennessee: Discipleship Resources, 1993), p. 13. (The contents of the book include models, workshops and training for mentoring ministry in the local church.)
[48] Effective Christian Education, p. 41.

church models hospitality in ways that children and youth know they are valued persons.

Difficult and yet perhaps very productive in the long term is refashioning some of our celebrations in a way that place children at the center. Here the reader is directed to a most helpful work, *Biblical Perspectives on Evangelism*. The author, the renowned biblical scholar Walter Brueggemann, argues for focusing on three groups of people as primary constituencies for evangelism. First and most obvious are the outsiders. Not to be overlooked are two other groups: jaded insiders, and "the children of believers who may or may not grow up to become consenting adults."[49] He emphasizes the importance of modeling a way for children to see faith lived out. In a Jewish home, he reminds us, children are not observers of an adult celebration but active participants. Indeed, the whole point of the celebration of Passover is to incorporate children into the miracle of the redemption of God's people. A communal church provides models, often in celebrations, for children to see the faith and hospitality lived out.

Examples of Shared Ministries with Children

A visit by one of the authors revealed a church where hospitality to children was especially evident. The children were valued not only by their own families but by the whole family of families.

A different family each time was invited to prepare the Communion elements. If the family included children, they too participated in the ministry. (Some churches include children in bringing forward the elements for communion.) At this same church, a visitation team was formed to make monthly calls on persons who were shut in. One team includes a couple and their two children who sing hymns and engage in conversation with the persons being visited. Another team is composed only of youth.

A young woman from New Zealand spoke of her family as the key to her faith journey. They served in many areas of ministry through the church. Her parents always took her with them. What was most important, however, was that they always encouraged her to help, to serve in a meaningful, age-appropriate way.[50]

In one city, numerous churches and synagogues participate in Room in the Inn, a ministry to homeless people. During the winter months, a particular church provides evening and morning meals, fellowship time, a bed, and a place to wash up. It is not uncommon for children to help serve meals and, together with their parents, eat with the people who are homeless.

---

[49] Walter Brueggemann, *Biblical Perspectives on Evangelism: Living in a Three-Storied Universe*. (Nashville: Abingdon Press, 1993), p. 94.
[50] This was the witness of Jennifer at a Lay Witness Global Gathering at Lake Junaluska, North Carolina in June, 1994.

In each of these examples we see two important functions taking place. First, the communal church is, significantly and meaningfully, extending hospitality to children in ways that enable them to experience welcome, belonging, and discipling. In addition, the communal church models for families ways they, too, can participate in faith sharing through the extending of hospitality within their household.

What difference would it make if the congregation, in its planning and visioning systems, understood the critical importance of family and the changing nature of the family? Are there times when the scheduling of ministries in the church contributes to fragmenting the families and adds frustration to family scheduling? Are there examples of the communal church itself working against the family being a domestic church?

SINGLES

The emphasis on the family as the domestic church also places high value on single persons. Chris is a single clergy person. He has discovered that when a pastor-parish relations committee explores the possibility of his coming to be with them, their questions do not always focus on his gifts for ministry nor on the leadership skills and qualities he possesses. Rather, he finds that the overt and hidden questions often are focused on the fact that he is single.

Kathy is another single clergy person. She, too, finds singleness is often an issue for the churches to which she is appointed. One of the things both of them have found when they begin a new ministry is that one of the first things people want to do is to take on the role of matchmaker for them. Both Kathy and Chris experience themselves as whole persons, satisfied and settled as singles. Often, in our valuing of marriage, we imply by the messages of our actions that single people are not whole and cannot have valuable and valid lifestyles, that they are less than who they should be.

Recently a cassette tape, focusing on pastors and "workaholism," arrived in our office. While it was never specifically stated, the underlying premise seemed to be that all pastors are married. Recommendations were made for writing firm commitments on the calendar for time with God. The only other suggestions for calendaring non-work time was for spouse and children. There was no recognition of the growing number of single clergy.

The communal church, as it looks at the variety of family and household configurations, will need to look carefully at the needs of single persons as well as to examine carefully its own stereotypes and attitudes toward persons and lifestyles of those who are single and settled. Perhaps a focus group of single people in different states of singleness could help examine what is said in the church in subtle (and sometimes not so subtle) ways about family and singleness. What is said in newsletters and in programming? What are the examples that are given in the sermon about significant relationships and about family and household?

Sometimes in families where there is divorce, children rotate between the parents on weekends and are not able to be in the same Sunday school class each week. In what ways do the teachers of children's Sunday school classes in your church help children from those families understand that they are full and valued members of their class? Some churches have added major Christian education experiences to a weekday after school. How does your congregation give support to single-parent families and help the single parent to be welcomed by the faith community in his or her new life situation? How does your church help the person who has lost a spouse in death to be welcomed and to belong once again?

DAILY RITUALS AND SYMBOLS IN FAMILY LIFE

Earlier in this chapter we talked about the importance of rites, symbols, and rituals in faith formation. According to Robert E. Webber, "external rites have the power to order an inner experience. This principle, which unites external action and internal reality, is rooted in the Christian doctrine of incarnation."[51] In the church building there are focal points and symbols that assist us in worship as we participate in rites and rituals. The domestic church would also be enriched in its faith formation if it, too, would have sacred spaces and symbols.

Celebrations in Ordinary Time

For some who love nature, sacred space could be a place outdoors, or it could be a space within the house reserved for quiet times. Works of art or symbols of Christ and the faith can often assist. Sacred space can be where all in the household gather as well as being a space that individuals might use. The light of a candle might be a reminder of the presence of God, the Light that enlightens the world and our lives. Some use the candle while traveling or sometimes even at work.

One family has a container on the table and once a day when they each have a meal together, they each talk about something for which they are grateful, or about a joyful moment that happened during the day. Then they put an offering in the container. When the container is full, the family members take turns suggesting the kind of ministry for which the money will be used.

---

[51] Robert E. Webber, *Celebrating Our Faith* (San Francisco: Harper & Row, Publishers, 1986), p. 8.

In the Judeo-Christian tradition, the domestic church is a place for sharing blessings with one another and for the telling of stories in ways that help persons see the intersection with God's story. Birthdays can be wonderful times for the sharing of blessings, for affirmation, for encouragement. Beverly's special gift to family members on their birthday is a poem she writes. Many of her poems are kept in special shoe boxes or other places where the persons who have received them retrieve them and read them again and again.

Celebrations of the Christian Year

Many families and households have begun to look at ways they can make celebrations of the Christian year such as Christmas and Easter truly celebrations of holy days. Instead of spending money on gifts for each other, some have made decisions as a family to take a few days of vacation time to spend quality time together, including a focus on the meaning of the Christian celebration.

Joanne, Tom, Becky, and Brent find a time when they can put up the Christmas tree together. They each take turns putting on an ornament and retelling the story of the ornament and why it is meaningful to them. They have a meal together and make it truly a family time.

During Advent and Lent some families and households make a covenant to spend time each week in a serving ministry with others. Members of the household take turns making suggestions of what that might be. Part of the decision-making process includes their faith commitment and how their relationship to the living Christ affects what and how they serve.

Offering Resources to the Domestic Church

During worship in Advent many churches have lay persons light candles of an Advent wreath. In your congregation, what are the family and household configurations represented by the persons lighting the advent wreath and praying the prayers?

Many churches have Advent and Christmas workshops to help families and households in their celebrations as the domestic church. This often includes making Advent wreaths together. Then they share rituals that can be used in the home as the candles are lighted. Others make chrismons and tell the stories of the symbols. In many of these workshops, families and households create crèche scenes and work together to help households develop their own symbols and rituals for these holy days.

In some traditions, the communal and domestic church join in the celebration of Epiphany, January 6, symbolizing the arrival of the magi in Bethlehem.

What resources does your congregation offer to the domestic church in faith formation during Lent?

Traditionally, Lent has been a time for people to deprive themselves of something. In the history of the early church, the giving up had more to do with persons making an intentional effort to live more simply, to give away and give up in order that their lives would not be controlled by things and possessions. It was a particular time in the Christian year to draw persons back to a life of simplicity and service in ways that helped to form and re-form them into the image and likeness of Christ. Some families and households, as part of their Lenten journey, focus on the message of Jesus as he read the scripture in the temple:

> *"The Spirit of the Lord is upon me,*
> *because he has anointed me*
> *to bring good news to the poor.*
> *He has sent me to proclaim*
> *release to the captives*
> *and recovery of sight to the blind,*
> *to let the oppressed go free,*
> *to proclaim the year of the*
> *Lord's favor"*
> *(Luke 4:18-19).*

They focus not only on growing in Christ toward a more simple lifestyle but also on participating more fully in the ministry to which Christ was called and, in turn, to which we are called as disciples of the living Christ.

SUMMARY

How does the communal church offer resources to the domestic church in order that the family and household might be the church? First, the life lived together in the communal church reflects a listening, caring, forgiving, and reconciling life among its members and as it reaches out to share the gospel in the world. The life of the congregation must reflect being the church of Jesus Christ in the way it tells and retells the story, in the way it shares faith and helps persons share faith, and in the way ancient Israel piled stones as symbols so children would ask, "Why are those stones piled there?"

In order to experience transformation and healing, persons must first experience a place where they can take off their masks and begin to tear down their own walls. In order to be able to do that, the place must be one in which trust is experienced, trust that one does not need to pretend to be someone else, trust that one can share weaknesses and strengths and be accepted by the community. This serves as a symbol and expression of God's acceptance and love. As the congregation models a place of hospitality and welcome, families and households also learn how to struggle and live together as a Christian community and learn how to be a place of welcome.

The communal church reflects its understanding of what it means to live together as people of God, both invited into the reign of God and invited to be co-creators with God in moving toward God's vision for the world. In the total life of the vital congregation, faith sharing is modeled both within and outside the church so families can observe and learn how to experience faith sharing as normative in their lives .

Second, the communal church can rediscover ways to help the family and household experience itself as a domestic church, constantly aware of its role in Christian faith formation. One way is to encourage the recovery of the ritual of house blessing. A sample of a house blessing is found in *The United Methodist Book of Worship*. We as authors both have had house blessings for our own homes and have either adapted other services or written our own. Both invited friends to participate with them in the service. In both cases candles were used to symbolize God's presence. The services also included the breaking of bread in fellowship and, for one, included the sharing of Holy Communion.

The house blessing can also be a way of sharing faith by having friends present who are not part of any church. Again, the remembering of the ritual brings to present time the commitment and covenant made with God, in the presence of friends, concerning the use of the home and space in ways that expressed hospitality even to "strangers." That we have been welcomed home in God is reflected for us in this act. The remembrance is a calling forth of the holiness of the ordinary space to our present being.

Third, a congregation can invite households and families to share and vision with one another ways in which the church can encourage and assist the family in positive practices of faith formation. Recently one family told how they spent time in family conference and extended dinner times to form a family mission statement. They tried to answer the question, "What is it we are about as a family?"

The faith-sharing congregation, in faithfulness to its Judeo-Christian heritage and in faithfulness to the One who was and is generous in grace, will invite and call forth families and households to be the domestic church!

GETTING STARTED

*"Few, if any, forces in human affairs are as powerful
as shared vision."*
Peter Senge, in The Fifth Discipline[52]

In previous chapters we have described what a faith-sharing
congregation might look like. Briefly, a faith-sharing congregation
is a vital congregation, focused on people yearning for God, finding God, being equipped and sent out to serve God by serving
people's needs. What enlivens any congregation is neither related
to activity level nor to the size of the membership. Vitality in congregational life has at least four component parts.

FOUR SIGNS OF A VITAL, FAITH-SHARING CONGREGATION

First, a vital or faith-sharing congregation heralds the good
news of the coming and eternal presence of God's Messiah in
Jesus Christ to inaugurate God's reign of shalom.

Secondly, such a congregation, like an alive and healthy person,
is in motion. When a person stops moving, he is usually dead or
close to it. People within a lively congregation are not static. There
is an "evangelical flow" of persons into and out of the congregation, gathering and scattering in worship and service. In such a
congregation this movement is persons, families, and households
daily living out the good news of Jesus by a weekly ritual of coming and going that supports a lifetime spiritual journey.

---

[52] Peter M. Senge, *The Fifth Discipline.*(New York: Doubleday/Currency, 1990), p. 206.

A third indicator of a vital congregation is that a spiritual leader is in charge. In a vital congregation such a leader will focus primarily on the equipping of the people for ministry within and mission beyond the congregation. "Without every-member ministry," writes R. Paul Stevens and Phil Collins, "we have unlived biblical truths, unstrategic leadership deployment, untapped resources in the congregation, and an unreached world."[53] Effective pastoral leaders will go beyond the traditional role of pastoral caregivers. They actually are more in the tradition of Moses than of Aaron, more prophet than priest. Such leaders are in charge, as Moses was, of the whole of congregational life and not just, as with Aaron, of the "religious" or worship life.

A vital or faith-sharing congregation, finally, is one in which innovative action is taken to "do the gospel" in new ways. Ministry and mission happen in such a congregation, very often in new ways. A small membership church in south Georgia began an after-school ministry to children in an effort to reach girls and boys not normally in Sunday school. Every Wednesday afternoon more than forty children were dropped off by school buses at the church for a two and a half hour period. Snacks were provided, as well as a quiet place for children who had homework to do. There was also recreation time and a forty-five minute "Sunday school" class! Today, in addition to Sunday school, that congregation has a Monday and Wednesday after school Christian education ministry. "New" children are targeted and are now coming with their parents and siblings on Sundays.

A vital congregation, like the one above, is one in which the positive experience of congregational life serves as an evangelist of the good news of Jesus. A vital congregation "heralds" or evangelizes Christ in the manner in which it initiates people into the kingdom of God. Faith is shared through hospitality, through equipping persons to share their faith, and through the offering of resources to families to feed and tend one another as a domestic church.

We have arrived at the point in this book where our concern is how to get started toward being a faith-sharing congregation.

THE IMPORTANCE OF LEADERSHIP

Ancient wisdom connects vision to growth. Without leaders God's people cannot prosper. Just to mention Moses and Paul is to make the case for the critical importance of leadership in moving God's people forward into new realities.

Sometimes it helps to think in different categories. Think of your congregation as a football team. Who is the pastor-leader?

---

[53] R. Paul Stevens and Phil Collins, *The Equipping Pastor* (The Alban Institute, 1993), p. XI.

Is he the water boy, the team physician, or the quarterback? None of the above! The pastor is the coach. As this metaphor illustrates, the pastor-leader is not the star player in the congregation. The coach is responsible for the whole team, for the way the players interact with each other on the field. A winning coach is also the principal cheerleader. As with everyone who excels in any task, winning coaches are students of their game. They are always learning new plays, new procedures for physically and mentally strengthening players as well as motivating them. Continuous learning and improvement is the goal of every coach. Just as a team needs a learning leader, a congregation will not share its faith effectively if their leader fails to be learning. To learn leaders read, attend workshops, and counsel with their colleagues in an effort to improve their performance.

In Exodus 18 Jethro outlines for his son-in-law, Moses, just what the role of a leader is. When Jethro saw Moses doing alone everything that needed to be done in the Hebrew camp, he spoke frankly: "'What you are doing is not good. You will surely wear yourself out, both you and these people with you'" (Exodus 18:17-18).

In the counsel he offers, the priest of Midian outlines the role of a spiritual leader as being three-fold. It involves staying close to God. "'You should represent the people before God'" (Exodus 18:19b). It also includes selecting persons to manage the affairs of the community. Moses is counseled to choose able persons "'who fear God, are trustworthy, and hate dishonest gain'" (Exodus 18:21). The centerpiece of Jethro's instructions is that Moses will regularly address the people on the subject of God's command and will: "'teach them the statutes and instructions and make known the way they are to go and the things they are to do'" (Exodus 18:20). Moses is counseled, as a leader, to keep the community centered on the vision of the community God wants.

BUILDING A SHARED VISION

There is much that a pastor can do on his or her own to move toward a faith-sharing congregation. The pastor can certainly be more personally intentional in hospitality to strangers, although pastors don't usually lack in that area. The pastor could also gather and teach a class in faith sharing as well as to focus more sharply in a personal ministry to families and family life. In other words, a pastor can do that much and then stop. The danger is the movement may stop there, as a personal rather than a congregational lifestyle. A common failing of many leaders is that they fail to lead by equipping others to do what they envision as needing to be done. This propensity to "go it alone," common among pastors, disenfranchises the congregation from meaningful ministry and rarely leads to long-term or systemic change.

The issue is building ownership or a shared vision in the congregation. One of the most passionate and persuasive visions in the 20th Century was verbalized by a black Baptist preacher on the mall in Washington, DC in 1963. "I have a dream," proclaimed Dr. Martin Luther King, Jr., "that one day on the red hills of Georgia, the sons of former slaves and the sons of former slave-holders, will be able to sit down at the table of brotherhood."[54]

There is a difference between a mission and a vision. King's "dream" was really a visionary statement. One of the distinguishing characteristics of a true leader is the ability to articulate and to promote vision. A mission is the work to which we have been called, to evangelize, and to make Christian disciples. A mission marks the boundaries of work. A mission rarely, however, sounds the trumpet to march forward. King's mission, you might say, was to end racial discrimination in this country. His vision, however, called people to make a decision, to answer "yea" or "nay." Unlike a mission, a vision is something you can see. A mission is intellectual; a vision is something you can see in your mind's eye.

Vision is also future centered. King's vision pulled a people to a new future—very much unlike their past—and to a better future for the nation as a whole. "Where there is no vision," the Bible says, "the people perish" (Proverbs 29:18, KJV). This is because neither the nostalgic pull of the past nor the assent to the status quo promises to renew or redeem the present time. Only a vision has that potential. In addition to being visual and future-centered, King's vision was also specific and attainable. It answers the questions: when ("one day"), where ("on the red hills of Georgia"), who ("the sons of former slaves and sons of former slave-holders"), and what ("will be able to sit down at the table of brotherhood"). Today it is still a powerful vision.

Yet as eloquent and passionate as King's "I Have a Dream" speech was, it could not of itself set a people's feet to marching on the long road to freedom. The fact is, the vision was not King's alone. Dr. King gave voice to the vision. He was the song's singer but not its composer. Two hundred years of oppression had written the song deep in the heart of black America.

The vision was a shared vision. Everyone that day in Washington made the vision his or her own. Because it was shared, people found the courage to act, knowing that they would not be acting alone. Without a doubt, the successful movement of a people from oppression to freedom in America (and in South Africa as well) is due, first and foremost, to shared vision. Shared vision compels people to act, disregarding the risk and sacrifice involved.

There is often with such a powerful and passionate vision an urgency to act immediately, to do something, to "strike while the iron is hot." In congregations, such passion can prompt premature birth. Leaders may act before the congregation or community has had the time to inwardly incorporate the vision as a shared vision. It is not uncommon for pastoral leaders to be under such compelling conviction that they make action decisions on their own while appealing for support from members of the congregation. Often the support is given, but sometimes the support is withheld because the leader, acting alone, has gotten out so far in front of the congregation as to appear to be the enemy. When a pastor goes it alone, the particular ministry rests in the hands of the leader. It appears to be his or hers alone. Others may assist, and it might prosper so long as the leader is in charge, but remove the leader in a pastoral transfer and very often the ministry goes as well.

In summary, the role of a Christian leader is critical to the development of a faith-sharing congregation. Leadership is to congregation what "location" is to real estate. Most important for leaders is to have a personal vision, to have the listening and communication skills to hear the hopes and dreams of the people, and to shepherd an integrative process that leads to ownership or shared vision. The role of the leader is not to play the martyr/hero, sacrificing self by doing everything that needs to be done in the name of the kingdom of God. It is a shared vision which leads to shared ownership, which, in turn, releases ministry in others.

The combination of the leader and congregation building a shared vision together is a critical factor in developing a faith-sharing congregation.

One way to cultivate this shared vision and to release ministry in others is to follow three steps: conviction, communication, and commencement.

I. CONVICTION

First there is a conviction or a need. In the northeastern United States, the rapid growth of one congregation threatened the sense of the covenant community which the people in the congregation, as well as the pastor, valued most in their church. Everyone knew one another and cared for one another. Lifelong friendships had been established. Needs were met through close relationships with members and pastor.

Growth, however, was bringing about changes. As the congregation grew larger, a second service was added and a second staff person—in Christian education—was hired. Both these actions stimulated more growth. More growth prompted more staff to be

hired. A third service was inaugurated. The congregation continued to grow.

George Parsons and Speed B. Leas have written about the
"tyranny of successful habits." "The seeds of decline," they write,
"are found in our successes."[55] Congregations get stuck in pat-
terns of responses to issues and problems. This congregation
needed a new paradigm for ministry. Members were experiencing
a loss of the intimacy which had attracted them to the congregation in the first place. The participation level of individuals in the
congregation was also diminishing as staff persons were hired for
functions once cared for by individuals or teams of church members. People began to talk about their "problem." It was, they
admitted, a good problem, but one that needed to be resolved.

To continue to grow was, they believed, in alignment with
God's will. But they also believed that the church was meant to
be a community in which people cared for each other and for
each other's faith journey. More and more people came under the
conviction that the role of the pastor was to lead and to offer
resources and equip persons for the day to day work of ministry
within and beyond the congregation. The conviction was in
alignment with what they took to be the primary task of the congregation. They wanted themselves to be an inviting, nurturing,
celebrating, and sending fellowship.

During a spring weekend the church council met for a planning
session. Members were asked to describe how they saw the congregation God wanted them to be. After a day of discussion, participants began to picture a congregation that heralded Christ, not
only in vital preaching and worship but also in the quality of
Christian fellowship in small groups. The image that began to
form in their minds reminded the charter members of the close fellowship they experienced when the church was young. People
began to get excited about a possibility that had not occurred to
them previously. As a large church they could still experience a
close community. Members would study and pray together as
small groups, supporting each other in their Christian life. They
would help one another to minister to persons with needs, and to
witness and offer invitations to unchurched friends and neighbors.

The planning group decided to model what they had been
talking about. The rest of the weekend was spent in small groups,
seeking further clarity. By the end of the planning weekend it
was clear that the church they envisioned was, indeed, the body
of Christ constituted, like a human body, by cells or small groups.
The principal learning from the small group discussion was the
need for trained small group leaders. Eventually, as these leaders

---

[55] George Parsons & Speed B. Leas, *Understanding Your Congregation as a System.* (The Alban
Institute, 1993), p. 1.

were trained, they were given the title of "lay ministers of pastoral care."

A faith-sharing congregation has a vision of itself as a center of hospitality, about people needing people on their Christian journey, about evangelism as the work of all the people, clergy and laity, and about the family, however constituted, as the domestic church, the place where faith is formed.

In getting started toward a faith-sharing congregation, the pastor and the laity must be convinced of the validity and urgency of such a move. It needs to be more than a good idea or something to do. It must become the one thing needed to become what those Christians believe God is calling them to be as a community of faith.

II. COMMUNICATION

The starting point for the Gospel of the evangelist John is communication: "In the beginning was the Word" (John 1:1). Communication through Christ, the Word, was the way God's dream of a new world reached God's people. The very act of Creation was the result of God communicating the desire of God's heart. "'Let there be light,'" God said, "'and there was light'" (Genesis 1:3). Creation and Christ both testify to the power of God's word.

From its very beginnings, Christianity has been Word-centered in Christ and word-centered as a faith to be proclaimed. Christians are at their best not as caretakers of an institution but as storytellers, as missionaries and witnesses. In the Scriptures, all gospel-tellers relate the story in their own way. In each, however, there is the same central theme of God's love become visible in Jesus Christ. The story, in other words, is also a picture, which, in proclamation, people not only hear but see.

To evangelize is to communicate. "We've a story to tell to the nations,"[56] we sing. The gospel is shared by communication. Whether preaching, or teaching, or sharing our faith, or practicing what we preach, we are communicating.

In the rapidly growing congregation we have been describing, full discussion of the problems associated with its rapid growth was encouraged in council and committee meetings, as well as in coffee hours and in casual corridor conversations. Many different ideas and strategies were entertained. A decision was made not to act prematurely. No immediate solution was forthcoming or expected. Time was intentionally allotted for full communication. Every person is important in a faith-sharing congregation. In this case, everyone's input was solicited and respected.

---

[56] The *United Methodist Hymnal,* (Nashville: United Methodist Publishing House, 1989) p. 569.

Do you have a conviction about a faith-sharing congregation? Don't rush it. Talk about it. Pastors have a chance to pursue ideas in the sermon, a weekly forum to raise questions and issues and to build the foundations for a shared vision. The singularly most important communication tool for the pastor/leader is the pulpit, and its opportunity for preaching and teaching. Week after week a congregation waits, for the most part, to hear what the Spirit is saying. Through the words of the pastor the Spirit reaches hearts within the gathered congregation.

The vision of a faith-sharing congregation, for instance, suggests many possibilities for a year of preaching and teaching. The truth is, if the inner directive of the pastor is to share God's vision for the church as a hospitable, equipping, and resourcing center for personal witness and family life, a year will not provide time for all the themes that will suggest themselves.

How does the average pastor rate the places of leadership, preaching, and teaching? In a recent poll involving more than a thousand pastors, 53% claimed a gift for preaching and teaching. Leadership as a gift, however, was identified by only 6 percent of the pastors.[57] It follows from this study that, in the minds of many pastors, preaching and teaching are not of themselves leadership functions. Preaching and teaching can be viewed chiefly as moral or spiritual instruction, or as being primarily devotional and inspirational in nature and purpose. Preaching and teaching, however, that dare to announce God's vision for a particular congregation, and its place and task in the community, denomination, and world is prophetic leadership in the best sense of the word.

To engage in the kind of preaching that paints a word picture of the unique calling of a particular congregation, inviting people to own the vision, is to display the gift of leadership. When newcomers were moving westward across the American prairie, the role of the wagon master, we are told, was to determine each new day which direction was indeed west and how, that day, they could move in that direction. In the act of preaching, pastors have a similar opportunity each week.

Any movement toward change in congregational life requires the dedication of a substantial block of time—at least a year—from the initial vision to implementation. Impatience, however, is next in line behind the desire to "go it alone," in the catalog of the professional "sins" of the congregational leader. *Short-cuts short-circuit the process of building shared vision. Take time!*

The writer of the book of Hebrews defines faith, in part, by the ability to "hang in" for the long pull. Living the life of desert nomads, Abraham and Sarah, says the writer, "looked forward to

---

[57] George Barna, *Today's Pastors* (Regal Books, 1993), pp. 117-124.

the city that has foundations, whose architect and builder is God" (Hebrews 11:10). Yet, the writer adds, these men and women "died in faith without having received the promises . . . Therefore God is not ashamed to be called their God" (Hebrews 11:13, 16).

Faith is an antidote to impatience. Faith permits the leader to take time, to allow ideas and visions to reach full term. What may appear to some as "wasting time" is, in fact, a spiritual discipline and gift.

Building shared vision presupposes that everyone has an opportunity to contribute to the finished product. In the congregation we have been describing, the laity was asked what kind of person, in their opinion, would make a good small group leader. Women's circle groups, program area committees, youth, and Sunday morning congregations all submitted "profiles." The characteristics needed were down-to-earth and basic: a positive person, committed and caring, flexible and non-judgmental. Staff and council worked on the training component. Communication was first on the training agenda, the ability to listen and to hear what is really being said.

The logical extension of this process was the invitation to members of the congregation to nominate persons who fit the profile. Based on the size of the membership, it was determined that a person should receive eight nominations in order to be invited. The pastoral staff was given the right to veto any nomination as well as to make nominations themselves. Staff persons are often the first to know of issues which would make a nomination burdensome, as well as to know new persons with gifts for lay pastoral ministry.

Several points emerge from this case study. In the first place, a full year for the communication process is recommended. In that year a pastor can help the congregation, through preaching and teaching, to see what he or she sees the congregation becoming as a missionary people, offering Christ through hospitality, personal faith sharing and helping each family become a domestic church. There is time, also, to help people recall and claim their own faith story and the role that hospitality, personal witness, and family played in that story. Various program committees can be assigned parts of the vision to work on. The worship committee might design a hospitality system appropriate to the particular congregation. The evangelism committee might be asked to design a training system to teach church members the principles of personal faith sharing. The education committee might be given a similar assignment, helping families share their faith. As such designs emerge, they are presented to the administration council and the congregation. Final plans are approved by the council along with specific plans for implementation.

III. COMMENCEMENT

Making a start need not resemble a ribbon-cutting ceremony with marching band and long speeches by local political leaders. A small, committed group consisting of persons particularly interested or gifted in the new ministry area, with concern for and perhaps gifts for hospitality, personal faith sharing, and family life can be enlisted to coordinate all of the new ministries. What makes such a group different from committees is that they will begin to practice the new ministry.

Another case study might illustrate the possibility here. In this case the new ministry was an effort to recover the church's healing ministry. The pastor was convinced, along with a group of lay persons, of the validity of a ministry of healing in a local church. The pastor led a Sunday morning forum with a large number of people attending. Discussion centered on the biblical, theological, and psychological foundations for a healing ministry. At the end of the forum an invitation was extended for interested persons to become part of the small management group.

The goals of this management group were to further study the role of Christian faith in the healing of persons, and to model the healing ministry by offering it within the group. Twenty-one persons met for ten weeks. At the end of that period, these persons had both experienced a healing ministry firsthand and had become a prayer and support community. With this experience they were able to interpret the ministry as it was being introduced to the congregation in the months that followed.

Can you picture a small group in your congregation working on becoming a faith-sharing congregation? Consider the possibility of a nine-week experience in which the group will spend three weeks on biblical insights about each of the component parts: hospitality, personal faith sharing, and the family as the domestic church. Each week would include a centering exercise, a discussion of the biblical insights about hospitality, personal faith sharing, or the domestic church, followed by a commitment to practice a specific ministry the following week.

The centering would be around the theme of the particular meeting. If, for instance, the theme is hospitality, the group might be led to focus on the meeting of Abraham and Sarah with the three angels. They might explore the significance of Abraham being called out of prayer to attend to the needs of the strangers at his door. Sarah's laughter at the thought of pregnancy at her age might be a momentary and enjoyable diversion. Hospitality is incomplete without moments of fun.

From a centering exercise, a discussion could follow, looking at what kind of ministry of hospitality is needed in the congregation. The discussion might focus on the training of ushers or greeters.

Another evening might focus on reasons some persons become inactive members of the congregation. Other evenings could be devoted to ministry possibilities in regard to personal faith sharing and to the family being the church. The important thing is to keep the focus on the practical. Each week members of the group commit to implementing during the week what they discussed and learned. They "do" hospitality or faith sharing or something specific within their family or for another family. In other words, ministry occurs as well as learning. During the next gathering, time is allotted for sharing the experience of the week. The result after nine weeks will be a growing body of knowledge in the area of the new ministry and an experienced and committed group of persons to support the extension of such ministries.

SUMMARY

On the evening of August 28, 1963, the greatest demonstration for freedom in the history of the American nation was over. The crowds dispersed, aglow with the experience and determined to work, to pray, and to struggle together until freedom was a given in every city and state in the nation. The crowd left the nation's capital knowing that the goal would be achieved one small step at a time. Many would argue that thirty years later we have still to reach journey's end, but the nation has come a long way, one step at a time.

Whatever the vision, affecting positive change is slow work. When a football team begins each new season, their vision is to be a winning team. Their particular goal, however, as they run onto the field at the beginning of each game is to win that particular game. Every team member knows that winning is one step at a time. Each time the team huddles the objective is to gain yardage and in four downs to make a first down.

In closing, remember two bits of advice: stay cool, and have fun.

Stay cool because Christ is the head of the church and with us in all of our efforts, step by step, to be a vital congregation of faith-sharing disciples.

Have fun, as well. "If we left it to the Spirit," writes John Killinger, quoting Jerome Murphy, " there would be nothing in the churches but Jesus and dancing."[58] Christ is the head of the church and the Holy Spirit is the supplier of our every need. There are energy and gifts for ministry available for the asking. There are good friends, too.

We find these good friends within congregations. Unlike some others of the world's religions, Christianity is centered in the life of the congregation. The primary task of Christianity is carried

---

[58] John Killinger, *Leave It To The Spirit* (New York: Harper & Row,1971), p. 46.

out in congregations, congregations that welcome, nurture, equip, and send out disciples to make the world more loving and just. It follows that nothing is more important for Christian leaders to put their energies toward than re-vitalizing congregational life. We trust the strategies described and discussed in this book may be helpful to that end.

Appendix

*"We don't talk about servanthood in terms of social activism
and do-goodism. We talk about it in terms of the servanthood
of the Lord, who serves us, who is our servant. It is out of that that we
minister to people . . . It comes out of being served."*
Norman Neaves, Church of the Servant, Oklahoma City[59]

As part of the research for writing this book the authors wanted
to go to a church that was a model of the faith-sharing congregation. There are certainly many such congregations large, medium,
and small, that provide a faith-sharing community for people. We
chose Church of the Servant as a congregation where we would
spend time. During one visit at Church of the Servant, we met
both with Pastor Neaves and with laity gathered in a focus group.

The laity in the focus group talked about why they were part
of Church of the Servant and the theology they experienced there.
The pastor talked to us about the theology of space, hospitality,
and creation as foundational for both their identity and their ministries. We share the experience of our visit in interview form.

Author: *What is it about Church of the Servant that has drawn*
you here?

Response 1:   I have been known as the daughter of, the wife of,
the mother of, but I have never had my own identi-
ty. I want to be known as a person, in my own right.

---

[59] Norman Neaves, pastor of Church of the Servant, Oklahoma City, Oklahoma, in interview
February 21, 1994

At Church of the Servant I have been accepted for who I am. This is the second time in my life I have been part of a church where I had the feeling I was truly part of a church family.

Response 2: When I came I felt alienated. I was divorced after 25 years of marriage. It was very painful for me. My children were not speaking to me; I had lost most of my friends; and I was alienated from my church where I had been for 50 years. I talked to one of the pastors here to see if I would be accepted. No one asked why I was divorced, why this, why that. The pastor saw gifts in me and said, "Why not use your gifts here." The staff and church have brought out the best in me. I am now a member of the care ministry.

Response 3: I didn't want to say to myself that I was Christian and was embarrassed to talk of myself as a Christian. I joined Church of the Servant. The deeper I got, the more honestly I began to look at who I was. I began to turn to the Bible. I began to see how the Bible applies to life; now the Bible and Jesus relate to every day. I am involved in ministries, and, like others who have come, want to give back what I have received.

Response 4: There had been so many sorrowful things happen in my family. I lost my grandson in a drowning; my daughter was in a 12-step program. My first Sunday in church Norman preached about someone being angry at God. That was a new concept. I had built up anger. I kept coming back to church. There is healing here. I had always had a hard time trusting people, even God. Here I feel safe.

Response 5: This has been a nurturing place. There has been a dramatic transformation in my life. I have moved from a two-dimensional life (mental and physical) to a four-dimensional life (adding spiritual and emotional).

Response 6: We had a two-and-a-half year old baby The people in the nursery understood feelings and seemed to know what was going on with me when I took our child there for the first time. The woman wanted to tell us all about what to expect and what would take place. There is an intentional one-on-one relationship in the nursery. One person takes care of the baby for the whole time. When I came to pick up the baby, they wanted to tell me all that had happened to her. It is reassuring and comforting not to have to worry about what is happening with the baby so my husband and I can go to church.

Response 7: Each Sunday the sermons challenge us to live out our Christianity. Before, I heard about and was taught about beliefs. Now beliefs are part of every-day living. There is always someone to eat with Sunday noon here at the church. That is really important to me. I meet someone new every time.

Response 8: The first Sunday at church the woman next to me asked me to join her at the Prime Time program (for persons over 50). She told me where and when to meet her. The group accepted me, and gradually encouraged me to take responsibilities in the group. It was the first time I had been in any kind of leadership role. I came alone and have more friends here than in my whole life before.

Response 9: Church of the Servant is a safe place. I told a friend who had been raped about the healing service at our church. When she arrived in the parking lot, she said to someone, "I'm not very dressed up. Will I feel strange here?" "No, you'll feel wel-comed" was the response. In the healing service she asked the pastor if there was any way she could be blessed without being touched. The pas-tor was sensitive to her request. There was accep-tance and safety.

Response 10: I have been given a ministry. I love plants and am responsible for caring for the plants outside the prayer chapel. It is important that the people who do the prayer ministry walk by plants that are well cared for and tended.

Response 11: My life was just not working. I needed power to live, not just another interesting lecture. I do not feel comfortable in large groups, but that is not a problem here. I did not know how to pray. In the healing service people pray with you. There is a prayer ministry where counselors and mentors help give you the rudimentaries.

Response 12: We were impressed with the outreach of the church.

Response 13: I work at the welcome center and reception desk. The church puts smiles on faces. The church has made a difference in helping me to be a decent, caring person and presence in my family. There are role models here. I can see what I want to be and can see myself becoming.

Author: *We have heard stories of profound welcome and transformation. What are the constituent parts of hospitality for you? What typifies welcome?*

Response 1: I did not come through the yellow pages. I came because of someone else. There was a sense of welcome in the stories told about Church of the Servant.

Response 2: I came through the friendships I developed on the softball team. The team was a cohesive, supportive group. They were the same on the field as in church.

Response 3: I visited one Sunday and was called by phone the next night. People continued to make contact. I felt like I was guided to a commitment.

Response 4: The top man sets the environment for what the company becomes.

Response 5: There is a welcome environment and outreach. It is Norman, but it is also present throughout the whole church.

Response 6: The music ministry is awesome. The music is part of welcoming and is deeply, deeply spiritual. There is great diversity in what takes place and persons of all ages are involved. That is welcoming.

Response 7: All occurs with basic Christian foundations. It is profound but simple and basic.

Author: *What can you say about the theology of the church?*

Response 1: The focus is on original goodness, not original sin. That provides acceptance. If you come with a theology of original sin, you beat up on yourself. There is an emphasis on what we can be and on acceptance.

Response 2: The church is a living example of Jesus Christ. There is acceptance, concern, care, forgiveness, love.

Response 3: Salvation is coming home to who we are.

Response 4: Norman is the vision-bearer.

During the interviews with the focus group and in conversations with staff and volunteers in the church there seemed to be four primary factors identified that made Church of the Servant a faith-sharing congregation. They were:

1. *Visionary leadership*
2. *Spirituality*
3. *Hospitality and welcoming where persons found*
    a. *a safe place*
    b. *acceptance*
    c. *a theology of goodness based on creation against a backdrop where sin, brokenness, and alienation are acknowledged*
    d. *hospitality and faith-sharing seen and experienced as the ministry of the whole congregation*
4. *Identification of and use of spiritual gifts and gifts for ministry encouraged*

We spent time with Norman Neaves and asked questions about leadership and theology of space. In order to understand some of the dialogue, we need to describe the worship space and gathering area. In the gathering area there is a large waterfall. Trees, plants and flowers are in abundance. The hallway opens to two floors, giving an impression of openness and space. There are many places with clear glass that open to the outside so one can see the outdoors and be reminded of the graciousness of creation.

The worship space also includes a waterfall and pool which are sometimes used for baptism. Again, there are many trees, plants, and flowers. While it is a large space overall, it is designed in alcoves so groups of persons can experience a sense of intimacy and family. There is glass all around so one has the sense that the whole of creation is an extension of the worship space. The pulpit is raised. The choir, orchestra, and congregation sit in pews that form a three-quarter circle. This gives people an opportunity to see faces and experience themselves to be part of a group. They are not just looking at the backs of heads. On the same level with the front pews and in the center is a half tree trunk which is the communion table and place of prayer. It is open with no railing or other barrier to the people approaching it.

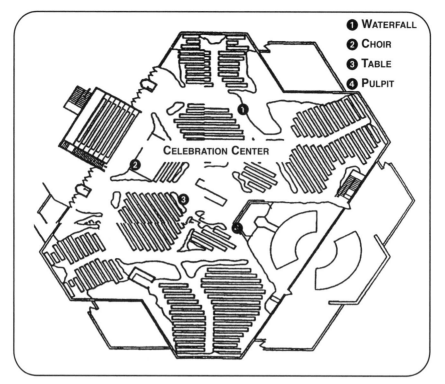

1 WATERFALL
2 CHOIR
3 TABLE
4 PULPIT

CELEBRATION CENTER

The following is part of our dialogue with the pastor about leadership and the theology of space:

Author: *What do you see as your role?*

Norman: When there were fewer members, I saw my role as doing everything. As the church grew I felt myself being displaced from that position. Now I see myself as the person who sees and shares the vision. I am not responsible for each part, but I have a picture of the whole and am responsible for seeing the whole.

Author: *Space is so important, as you say. You've designed this space to raise your "family." Space will also influence what you become.*

Norman: We create the buildings, but they create us more than we create them.

Author: *At the first church site (The interview took place three months after they had moved into a new church building at a new site.) you called the place where people gathered the "celebration center." I don't see signs titling the space or directing people to the "celebration center" as I did at the other church. Are the people becoming "sanctuary" oriented?*

Norman: Rather than forcing names, we would like to let them emerge out of the experience of the people. For some people it's a "garden of faith." For others it is a "cathedral of creation." Others refer to it as "the oasis." Most people call it the "celebration center." Some have said this is the first time they like the word "sanctuary." They didn't like it before because it suggests that it is a retreat from the world. This space suggests to them more of an "oasis" and a "safe place" in the world.

Author: *We heard the image of "safe place" expressed several times with the focus group. What is it (sanctuary) to you?*

Norman: It is all of those things. Though we celebrate there, the problem I have with "celebration center" is the word "center." Center has an institutional sound to it. It sounds kind of functional. Celebration does describe in a functional way what we do there. But the place, for me, is so full of sacrament and the sacrament of creation. The place, for me, has a spirit of being. The Lord lives there. It's a sacrament of space, sacramental space. That is not to the exclusion of what's in the world. Because the space is so open to the world and brings the world in, it declares and makes evident the sacrament of all the world.

Author: *What is the focal point in the sanctuary?*

Norman: There is no focal point. That does not mean it's unfocused. Rather it is multi-focused. In most churches there is the "head" and the "box." Basically, to be polite you do not turn around and look someone in the face. You sit looking at the back of people's heads. In the box behind the altar railing, the music and the preaching are offered, and the sacrament is served. Everything comes from there to the people In the space here, at Church of the Servant, you sit in the midst. There's the choir; there's the orchestra; there's the table; there's the pulpit; there's the sky; there's the waterfall; there are the trees; there's a garden. The scripture is read in the midst of the congregation. The prayers are led from the congregation. Whoever preaches is in the pulpit, but all else happens in and through and with the congregation.

Author: *How did the church begin? How did you choose the name Church of the Servant?*

Norman: We began our church with a strong sense of the lowliness of God, focusing on the foot-washing episode in John 13. Servanthood was, when we formed, and it continues to be, even to this day, the pivotal image around which our whole church has developed. From that image we came to look upon God, not so much as the one who is above us, but rather as the one who is beneath us. I've always tried to point out that the word "servant" in the name of our church is not in the plural form. It's singular. And so our church is not "Church of the Servants" in the plural, but rather Church of the Servant in the singular. In other words, we're not the servant. The Lord is. Unless first of all we experience ourselves as having been served, we really don't have anything with which to serve or to offer to the world. The ministry that takes place in and through our church is the ministry of Christ himself, shared with us generously and abundantly. Now we have an opportunity to let it flow through us and to be shared generously and abundantly with others. If that were not so, we would not really be engaged in ministry so much as just social action or community support.

Author: *We have noticed that you use the word celebration rather than worship. What's the difference between celebration and worship?*

Norman: In my opinion, it's really the difference between the two Testaments. Basically speaking, the Old Testament moves from earth to heaven as in the Tower of Babel, whereas the New Testament moves from heaven to earth as in Bethlehem. It is not so much a matter of reaching upward to God as it is a matter of realizing that God reaches downward to us. And so when we gather as God's people, we do not gather to "worship" God as much as we gather to "celebrate" the good news that God has come and is among us and stoops way down to serve us even at our most basic and lowliest of points.

Author: *We saw that your communion table is on the level with the people, in their midst and is an unfinished tree trunk.*

Norman: The early church gathered in homes around a table made of wood reminding them of the cross. We call ours the table of the Lord. We don't just call it a communion table because it's more than that. We pray there. It's a place to meet the lowly One who is our friend. The early church didn't gather around an altar upon which to offer their sacrifices to the Lord so much as they gathered around a wooden table to celebrate the brokenness of Christ's body and thus, strangely, the atonement offered to everyone. And so it is that we have a table in the midst of our gathering space, not lifted up high like an altar, but down low with the people gathered around it.

Author: *It sounds to me like that's a very foundational theology for hospitality, in the sense that we're all standing at this level of having been served.*

Norman: To have the table in the midst of the people without a railing is a recovering of the sense of the gathered community of Christ in the home, around the table of the Lord, breaking the bread, sharing the cup, reminding us of the brokenness of God given to us. Our servant is the One who bridges the gap and declares himself to be for us forever. So we want it (the table) open. We don't want railings around it. It's free. It's accessible. It's touchable. It's all holy.

Author: *You have talked to us about the theology of space. One of the first things we noticed was the presence of waterfalls, trees, flowers, other plants, the view of the sky and outside, and the feeling of space, yet intimacy.*

Norman: There is a lot of touching in our church and we hold hands. This begins to get at what I really like to refer to as hospitality. It gets at the hospitality of the Lord, the generosity of the Lord given in the flowers, given in the trees, given in the sky, given in the water, given in one another. It's all connected; it's all related. It is a blessed world in which we live. It's all sacrament and we live in it. We are part of the sacrament.

It reminds me of a moment at the close of the service one Sunday when we were all holding hands and singing the Lord's Prayer. I happened to notice a man and his small son sitting on an aisle. I was so touched when I saw the little fellow holding his dad's hand with his own right hand and then reaching up to take hold of a palm branch with his free hand on the left. That little fellow understood that we are all connected, not just in the human family, but in the family of all of creation. He understood in a very primal and basic way that all of creation is a sacrament in which we are given the privilege of living our lives. That deep awareness and realization form the profound theological basis out of which a real ministry of hospitality is born and offered generously to everyone everywhere.

The foundational issues the pastor, Norman Neaves, shared with us are like those expressed by the focus group from the church and those outlined in the preceding pages. Some of the theological issues central to our conversations with Norman were:

1. The role of the leader as a visionary and spiritual leader is critical. The pastor's role is that of seeing and holding the vision and equipping the laity for their ministry.
2. A theology of hospitality grounded in the generosity of creation is foundational to the faith formation of individuals and the congregation.
   a. Hospitality is the role of the whole congregation.
   b. Hospitality means helping persons to be at home, to find a safe place, and to find their home in Christ.
   c. The theology of creation helps one to focus on the goodness and hope of original creation.
   d. The theology of creation helps one to remember the generosity and abundance of God.
3. It is important to help people identify and use their gifts.
4. The design and use of space is central to the experience of "being at home."

As we have described in these pages, God's self-revelation was given first to patriarchs, through the patriarchs to families, and then to the children. We affirm that the family, however constituted, is still the primary center of hospitality and faith formation. God's further revelation in Jesus Christ, however, has called us as families and households into a larger "family of families."

The authors have experienced this larger family in several local congregations, as youth and adults, and as professional leaders. Indeed, our description of a faith-sharing congregation is modeled after them. They have welcomed us, encouraged the use of our gifts for ministry, nurtured our relationship with God, and sent us into the world with a vision of God's shalom. These congregations have also supported our efforts to be, in our families and households, the domestic church.

It is our hope that, as pastors and leaders in congregations, you have had this same experience and, with us, will continue to hold, grow, and implement this vision for the sake of all those whom God loves and paid so dear a price to redeem.

Suggested Reading

HOSPITALITY
Keifert, Patrick R., *Welcoming the Stranger: A Public Theology of Worship and Evangelism* (Minneapolis: Augsburg Fortress, 1992).

Koenig, John, *New Testament Hospitality: Partnership With Strangers as Promise and Mission* (Minneapolis: Augsburg Fortress, 1994).

Nouwen, Henri J.M., *Reaching Out: The Three Movements of the Spiritual Life* (New York: Doubleday & Company, 1986).

Palmer, Parker J., *The Company of Strangers: Christians and the Renewal of America's Public Life* (New York: Crossroads, 1983).

Pohl, Christine D., *Making Room: Recovering Hospitality as a Christian Tradition* (Grand Rapids, MI: William B. Eerdmans Publishing Company, 1999).

Sweet, Leonard I., *Quantum Spirituality: A Postmodern Apologetic* (Dayton: Whaleprints, 1991).

FAITH SHARING
A Journey of Faith: Lay Witness Mission Handbook (Nashville: Discipleship Resources, 2000).

Crandall, Ron, *The Contagious Witness: Exploring Christian Conversion* (Nashville: Abingdon Press, 1999).

Crandall, Ronald K., *Witness: Exploring and Sharing Your Christian Faith* (Nashville: Discipleship Resources, 2001).

Fox, H. Eddie and George E. Morris, *Faith-Sharing: Dynamic Christian Witnessing by Invitation (Revised and Expanded)* (Nashville: Discipleship Resources, 1996).

Fox, H. Eddie and George E. Morris, *Faith-Sharing Video Kit* (Nashville: Discipleship Resources, 1996).

FAMILY AS DOMESTIC CHURCH
Brueggemann, Walter, *Biblical Perspectives on Evangelism: Living in a Three-Storied Universe* (Nashville: Abingdon Press, 1993).

Hays, Edward, *Prayers for the Domestic Church: A Handbook for Worship in the Home* (Easton, KS: Forest of Peace Books, 1989).

Pockets (Nashville: The Upper Room), a devotional magazine for children that is published monthly (except Jan/Feb).

Thompson, Marjorie J., *Family, the Forming Center: A Vision of the Role of Family in Spiritual Formation (Revised)* (Nashville: Upper Room Books, 1996).

LEADERSHIP
Covey, Stephen R., *The 7 Habits of Highly Effective People* (New York: Simon & Schuster, 1989).

Hunter, George G. III, *Church for the Unchurched* (Nashville: Abingdon Press, 1996).

Hunter, George G. III, *The Celtic Way of Evangelism: How Christianity Can Reach the West...Again* (Nashville: Abingdon Press, 2000).

Hunter, George G. III, *How to Reach Secular People* (Nashville: Abingdon Press, 1992).

Keck, Leander E., *The Church Confident* (Nashville: Abingdon Press, 1993).

Mead, Loren B., *The Once and Future Church: Reinventing the Congregation for a New Mission Frontier* (Bethesda, MD: Alban Institute, 1991).

Payne, Bishop Claude E. and Hamilton Beazley, *Reclaiming the Great Commission: A Practical Model for Transforming Denominations and Congregations* (San Francisco: Jossey-Bass, 2000).

Senge, Peter M., *The Fifth Discipline: The Art and Practice of the Learning Organization* (New York: Doubleday, 1994).

Shawchuck, Norman and Roger Heuser, *Leading the Congregation: Caring for Yourself While Serving the People* (Nashville: Abingdon Press, 1998).

Stevens, R. Paul and Phil Collins, *The Equipping Pastor: A Systems Approach to Congregational Leadership* (Bethesda, MD: Alban Institute, 1993).

Weems, Lovett H., Jr., *Church Leadership: Vision, Team, Culture, and Integrity* (Nashville: Abingdon Press, 1993).